DEATH BY
Chocolate
COOKIES

MARCEL DESAULNIERS
AUTHOR OF *DEATH BY CHOCOLATE*

Photography by Michael Grand

SIMON & SCHUSTER

SIMON & SCHUSTER

SIMON & SCHUSTER
Rockefeller Center
1230 Avenue of the Americas
New York, NY 10020

A KENAN BOOK

DEATH BY CHOCOLATE COOKIES
was prepared and produced by
Kenan Books
15 West 26th Street
New York, NY 10010

Editor: Nathaniel Marunas
Art Director/Designer: Jeff Batzli
Photography Director: Christopher C. Bain
Production Director: Karen Matsu Greenberg
SIMON & SCHUSTER Editor: Janice Easton

Color separations by Colourscan Overseas Co Pte Ltd.
Printed in Singapore by KHL Printing Co Pte Ltd.

1 3 5 7 9 10 8 6 4 2

Library of Congress Cataloging-in-Publication Data

Desaulniers, Marcel.
    Death by chocolate cookies / Marcel Desaulniers.
        p.   c.m.
Includes bibliographical references (p.   –   ) and index.
    1. Cookies.   2. Cookery (Chocolate)   I. Title.
TX772.D47   1997
641.8'654—dc21   96-54840 CIP
    ISBN 0-684-83197-X

DEDICATION
To those who served—
India Company, 3rd Battalion, 26th Marines

ACKNOWLEDGMENTS
Many thanks to the sweet folks who share my love for
confections and contributed to this delicious undertaking:

Connie Desaulniers
Jon Pierre Peavey
Dan Green
Michael Grand
Penny Seu
John and Julia Curtis
Kelly Bailey
Michael Holdsworth
Bill Rosen
Janice Easton
Nathaniel Marunas
Jeff Batzli
Chris Bain
Michael Friedman
Simon Green
Mrs. D
The students, instructors, and staff at the
Culinary Institute of America

CONTENTS

Notes from Ganache Hill

INTRODUCTION

I thought a cookbook that covered as much chocolate geography as this should have a title that suggests the universality of the subject, rather than something as obvious as *Death by Chocolate Cookies*. The title should scream out that chocolate is not just the most deliciously intoxicating substance in the cosmos, it might be the key to universal peace. Fortunately, I was brought to my senses (actually, my agent deprived me of chocolate for several weeks), and realized that a book that exalts hand-held chocolate treats needs to convey exactly that in its title.

My assistant Jon Pierre Peavey and I spent several months crafting the crunches, munches, lickings, nibbles, morsels, tidbits, goodies, chews, and even slurps included in this book. Rather than showcasing towering confections like those in *Death by Chocolate* and *Desserts To Die For*, this is a collection of chocolate cookies, bars, brownies, nougat, brittle, praline, ice-cream sandwiches, candies, and biscuits that you can hold in your hand and pop in your mouth. O.K., so I went overboard and pulled out the plates in the chapter "More Than a Mouthful." But as Mae West said, "Too much of a good thing is wonderful."

GANACHE HILL

When I asked my wife, Connie, in 1986 if she would mind my testing recipes for *The Trellis Cookbook* from our home kitchen, she enthusiastically assented.

As more books followed, however, so did the wear and tear on the kitchen. Connie never fussed as I and an assistant worked our way through five cookbooks, but it was obvious that if I wanted to continue creating more cookbooks, I needed to find an appropriate, less intrusive locale (thankfully, Connie never considered tossing me out).

That is how Ganache Hill came to be. After a lengthy search for a location near the Trellis, my partner John Curtis and I purchased a handsome piece of property four miles from the restaurant. Perched on a hilltop lush with herb and vegetable gardens, white pine, dogwood, magnolia, crepe myrtle, pecan, and oak trees, Ganache Hill is a sixteen-hundred-square-foot space that has everything I need—including home (not restaurant) equipment—to develop, test, and write recipes under one roof.

This cookbook is the first to be conceptualized, tested, and written at Ganache Hill. I hope you have as much fun reading and baking with *Death by Chocolate Cookies* as Jon Pierre and I had putting it together at our culinary paradise. I am looking forward to many more delicious book projects here on the hill.

JON PIERRE PEAVEY

If Holmes had been without Watson, I'm afraid the hound would have done Sherlock in. Likewise, I can't imagine creating a cookbook without my assistant Jon Pierre Peavey. Jon Pierre came to Williamsburg to work at the Trellis in 1988, directly from the Culinary Institute of America in Hyde Park, New York. I had recruited him a few months earlier with my standard disclaimer to culinary school students that the work would be hard, the money would not be grand, and advancement would be limited because of loyal staff. Rather than being deterred, Jon Pierre was energized by these challenges, and within a couple of years had been promoted to assistant chef. In 1993 when I began putting together *The Burger Meisters*, I enlisted Jon Pierre to work on the project.

Jon Pierre took to the process like hot cream to chopped chocolate; now he works full time with me on cookbooks and assists me with cooking demonstrations, special appearances, television shows, and many other undertakings.

HOUSEKEEPING

Mastering most of the recipes in this book requires only a little time and effort—though the recipes in the "More Than a Mouthful" chapter are admittedly challenging, especially Chocolate Mango Ambush—and a lot of love for chocolate. Although the recipes are straightforward, I enthusiastically recommend that you read them from start to finish before proceeding. Don't forget the equipment list and "The Chef's Touch." Variables exist in every recipe (mixing time and baking time, just to name a couple) and you will want to be aware of all steps of the recipe before starting so you can avoid the frustrating discovery that you are short of an ingredient or missing a critical piece of equipment midway through the baking process.

After reading the recipe and before you actually start baking, pull out all the necessary equipment so it is within easy reach. Organize and prepare all the foods listed in the recipe. In professional kitchens, this is known as the *mise en place*, a French term that translates to "put in place." Once you have assembled the ingredients as listed—this means measuring the flour, chopping the chocolate, cutting the butter into 1-ounce pieces, and so on—then it's time to start cooking.

Whether you are a fledgling baker or an accomplished master, it makes good sense to be careful in the kitchen. The potential for cuts and burns is ever-present when baking, so keep your knife sharp (ironically, most cooks cut themselves with dull knives), pay attention to what you are cutting, and keep a clean and dry towel nearby (the result of handling a hot pan with a damp or wet towel is, to say the least, stimulating).

You are no doubt tuned in to the latest governmental warning about what we eat and drink—and let's face it, life is dangerous. Being cautious about food handling makes serious sense. It didn't take a lot to convince me that consumption of raw eggs, which may contain salmonella bacteria, was not healthy (we now use pasteurized eggs for items like mousses at the Trellis). It is good common sense to wash fruits and vegetables before using them, to minimize surface bacteria and parasites. And don't forget to keep your hands clean!

OVENS

Although this is not the equipment section, I feel compelled by my desire to have you baking up a storm (and a few cookies) to discuss ovens early in the game. Baking has many variables: quality of ingredients (how old are those so-called fresh eggs?), weather conditions (that darn humidity), geography (not everyone likes a Rocky Mountain high), exact measurements (fifth-grade math was not my cup of tea), skill (practice makes perfect), and one of the more critical variables, your oven.

I have found that most home ovens are not properly calibrated (that is, the oven temperature is not in sync with the oven setting). A 20- to 25-degree-Fahrenheit discrepancy is not unusual. I recommend purchasing an oven thermometer at a kitchen supply store and relying on it for accuracy. During the testing of cookie recipes for this book, it became very apparent that even with a simple item like cookies, the oven temperature needed to be accurate for successful results.

Be sure to preheat the oven as directed. Starting off a batch of cookies in an oven that has not reached the proper temperature will yield mediocre or even disastrous results. If your oven capacity is limited (you can only fit one baking sheet on a rack) and you need to extend the baking process, make sure the oven returns to the designated temperature before placing the next flight of cookies in the oven. Also, opening and closing the oven door to peek at what is baking inside will affect the temperature.

To maximize your success at getting an evenly baked cookie, I often recommend switching the baking sheets on the racks in the oven as well as rotating the sheets 180 degrees about halfway through the baking time.

I will not recommend gas versus electric ovens, nor will I plug a specific manufacturer's brand, but I will tell you that I have found considerable differences in the refraction of heat (circulation of heat waves) in the ovens I have used. If you are interested in purchasing a new oven, I suggest that you talk to as many friends and acquaintances as possible, especially those who are bakers. Manufacturers market their products as the best, but I can tell you from experience that some of the big names don't always deliver the best quality. If you are interested in knowing which ovens we use at Ganache Hill (they are very accurate and the even flow of heat gives us excellent results), you can e-mail me (goganache@aol.com) and I will share that information with you.

INGREDIENTS

We always purchase the ingredients for cookbook recipe testing at local Williamsburg supermarkets (versus getting food-service–style products as we do at the Trellis). I believe it is the cookbook author's responsibility to the reader to test recipes using the same ingredients typically available to consumers, because while some items—for instance, milk, baking powder, and baking soda—do not vary between consumer products and commercial products, items like heavy cream, cream cheese, and chocolate purchased from a professional supplier differ greatly from those obtained in most retail stores. From experience, I believe a home baker can produce excellent baked goods with readily available products.

Most cities (Williamsburg included) have a specialty supermarket or upscale chain supermarket. I find that these types of retailers carry the widest variety of items like dried fruits, nuts, specialty flour (masa harina, for instance), and high-quality baking chocolate. Don't skimp on quality, since the end results are only as good as the ingredients purchased. The following is my short list of some of the more important ingredients used in this book. These ingredients are listed in alphabetical order—otherwise, chocolate would be first.

BUTTER

Invariably when I teach a cooking class I am asked many questions on the subject of butter. The typical question with regard to savory foods is: "Can I reduce the amount listed or eliminate butter altogether?" And, when asked about butter in relationship to sweets and baking in general, the question is usually: "Does it make a real difference if you use margarine or shortening instead of butter when you bake?" Both are valid questions. To the former question my answer is maybe. To the latter question, I answer unequivocally that it does make a difference. In both cases, it's a matter of flavor. For instance, with certain savory foods olive oil would be appropriate and butter need not apply. But for my money, when it comes to baking, nothing replaces the rich and lustrous flavor of butter. Margarine and shortening can be substituted in many baking recipes, but with variable results. The proportion of fat and water in butter versus margarine can affect the leavening, texture, and palatability of a baked good.

CHOCOLATE

Let's talk about my favorite fruit, the fruit of the cacao tree, which yields chocolate. All of the recipes tested for this book were produced using U.S.–manufactured chocolate that was purchased in Williamsburg supermarkets (no doubt we depleted local inventories while we were testing).

For more than twelve years we used a U.S. chocolate at the Trellis, but switched to French chocolate when the U.S. manufacturer discontinued production of 10-pound bars, leaving us with the choice of using tiny, individually wrapped 1-ounce bars or finding another source for the 300-plus pounds of chocolate we use weekly. The French chocolate manufacturer gave us a good deal, so the rest, as they say, is history.

U.S. chocolate manufacturers produce excellent chocolate. From the brands that are readily available in the supermarkets to the lesser-known brands found in specialty stores, I love them all. Well, almost all. Several American chocolate manufacturers are marketing products that I call "convenience chocolate." These chocolate-flavored items usually substitute tropical oils for the cocoa butter found in real chocolate and sometimes contain strange additives like carnauba (useful if you are planning to wax your car). My advice is to read the listing of ingredients on the label and be aware of the following characteristics:

Unsweetened Chocolate

The purest form of chocolate you can purchase, unsweetened chocolate should have just one ingredient: chocolate, sometimes listed as chocolate liquor. Unsweetened chocolate by composition is more than 50 percent cocoa butter; the remaining amount is made up of cocoa solids. It contains no sugar, vanilla, or other additives, making it bitter and inedible. To be consumed, it must be melted and used in a batter or dough that contains sugar. Sales of unsweetened chocolate are not exactly brisk, so look for boxes that seem to have been placed recently on the shelf (boxes that are not dusty or banged up are a good bet).

Semisweet Chocolate

Semisweet chocolate is the most frequently used chocolate in this book. Typically, the ingredients listed on the package will be unsweetened chocolate, sugar, vanilla or vanillin (an artificial flavoring), and lecithin (an emulsifier). I recommend that you purchase only as much as you need for the item you are preparing. Chocolate is susceptible to moisture and heat, so always store it in a cool, dry place (you can keep it in the refrigerator, as I do, if the chocolate is well wrapped). Bittersweet chocolate may be used in place of semisweet in any of our recipes, especially if you favor a more intense flavor. Bittersweet chocolate usually contains a higher percentage of cocoa solids, giving a deeper color and a more intense flavor.

White Chocolate

Why is white chocolate white? It contains no cocoa solids, only cocoa butter. Consequently, it has a chocolate flavor (albeit subtle), but no color. Read the list of ingredients on the package carefully; if cocoa butter is not mentioned, move on. (Especially beware of white chocolate labeled "white coating.")

Cocoa Powder

We use a fair amount of cocoa powder in this book. Cocoa powder is manufactured by removing most of the cocoa butter from unsweetened chocolate. Contrary to what some folks believe, there is some fat in cocoa powder because not all of the cocoa butter can be pressed out. Purchase unsweetened cocoa powder, not breakfast cocoa drink mix. The only ingredient listed on the package should be cocoa.

Chocolate Chips and Mini-Morsels

Who doesn't love chocolate chips? As lovable as they are, however, do not substitute chocolate chips in recipes calling for semisweet chocolate. Although quality chips and mini-morsels are manufactured from semisweet chocolate, the formulation is different. Someone recently wrote me for help in solving the problem of a favorite family fudge recipe gone bad: for years this recipe was made successfully, but now the results were mediocre. After a few questions, I learned that my pen pal had started using chocolate chips because they were more convenient than the semisweet chocolate called for in the recipe. Switching back to semisweet solved the problem.

EGGS

In every recipe where eggs are listed, I note large eggs (we use Grade AA large eggs and I urge you to do the same). The quality of eggs can make or break a baking recipe, so be sure to check the pull date on the carton and always buy fresh eggs. And remember, proper handling of eggs is not only important for making delicious food, it is fundamental for health reasons. Keep the eggs refrigerated in the carton. Any perceived benefit of using room-temperature eggs is outweighed by health considerations.

I also recommend washing your hands after you have handled eggshells. Don't keep separated eggs in the refrigerator for more than a day or two (make sure the eggs are tightly covered), and do not freeze separated eggs. And as tempting as it may be, do not eat dough containing raw eggs. A little precaution can go a long way toward preventing the possibility of salmonella poisoning.

FLOUR

I am a proponent of name-brand flour (Gold Medal and White Lily come to mind). We have found that high-quality flour has a look and feel that generic flours lack. Baking results can be affected by the use of poorly milled and packaged flour. The nominal cost differential aside (the name brands are obviously going to cost a bit more), I suggest using the best.

HEAVY CREAM

Ahh...whipping cream. Without this ingredient, the world would be a less delicious place, because then we would not have ganache. Of course, nothing prevents you from making ganache with milk, half-and-half, or even condensed milk—nothing, that is, but flavor. The velvety consistency and sensuous flavor of heavy cream is special. I would no more use anything other than heavy cream than I would use carob instead of chocolate.

We purchased ultra-pasteurized cream in the supermarket for testing the recipes in this book because it was readily available. At the Trellis we use fresh heavy cream, which has a shorter shelf life but a more voluptuous flavor than the ultra-pasteurized. Buy fresh if available, but I assure you the ultra-pasteurized will yield excellent results.

NUTS

I hope you're feeling squirrely, because a majority of the recipes in this book contain nuts. Every week at the Trellis we use more than two hundred pounds of nuts of all types in ice cream, cakes, cookies, and other dessert items, as well as in salads, main course items, and even as a garnish for several soups, including our corn and peanut soup. With that track record, it is not surprising that so many of the recipes in this book include a variety of nuts.

Nuts are less pricey since good supermarkets started including them in their bulk food departments. Once purchased, I recommend storing nuts in a cool, dry place (we store them in the freezer). Always toast nuts before using them to enhance both the flavor and texture.

SUGAR

Sugar is an essential element in the chemistry of baking. The silkiness of an ice cream, the crispness of a cookie, and the feel of a candy in the mouth are all affected by the amount of sugar used. Although some people try to limit sugar intake for important dietary reasons, others can consume a reasonable amount without any harmful effects. The amount of sugar in our recipes is just the right amount of sugar necessary to deliver the desired tastes and textures. You may experiment with reducing the amount of sugar in a recipe—we have, with mixed results. With items like ice cream and sorbet, decreasing the sugar will affect the texture and cause both items to get very hard. You have more opportunity for success in lowering sugar levels in baked goods. If you have dietary reasons for limiting sugar intake, consider experimenting with fructose, a natural substance derived from fruit that can be purchased in granulated form. The level of sweetness derived from fructose is ounce-for-ounce more intense than that of sugar (although some of the sweetness dissipates if it is heated).

Techniques & Equipment

TECHNIQUES

COOLING COOKIES

"Transfer the cookies from the baking sheet to a cooling rack." This instruction seems to be universal in cookie recipes. Is it necessary to do so? After Jon Pierre and I tested and evaluated over eighty recipes for this book, I have to answer that most of the time it does not seem to be necessary. It is simply more convenient to remove the cookies from the oven and allow them to cool on the baking sheets (unless you need the baking sheets for another batch of cookies) than it is to transfer hot cookies to a cooling rack. So if you are looking to save time, you can forgo the rack with the recipes in this book.

CUTTING BROWNIES AND BARS INTO PORTIONS

To cut 24 portions, leave the baked and cooled brownie or bar in the pan. Use a serrated knife with rounded tip to cut the brownie lengthwise across the center. Then cut each half lengthwise in half. Now make five cuts widthwise to make equal sixths. If you have any doubts, do a little sketch to visualize how cutting this rectangle three times across the length and five times across the width will yield 24 portions. It's really rather elementary—that is, unless you are like me and have no aptitude for geometry (I had help with this one).

INCORPORATING BUTTER INTO A DOUGH OR BATTER

The incorporation of butter into a dough or batter is an important element in the success of a recipe. For best results, use a table-model electric mixer and adhere to mixing times. For most of the recipes tested in this book, we used cold butter directly from the refrigerator, cut into 1-ounce pieces. For those exceptions where the butter needs to be at room temperature, instructions are specifically given.

MELTING CHOCOLATE

Slowly heating chocolate in a double boiler until it is melted and completely smooth is not a bad task—in fact, it is a delicious one. (I always help myself to a finger or two of chocolate while doing it.)

A double boiler is the piece of equipment I prefer for melting chocolate (other methods include the microwave, heating pad, or even an oven set on low heat). In essence, a double boiler is comprised of two pieces: a top (which holds the chocolate) and a bottom (which holds the water). You may fashion a double boiler by nesting a stainless steel or glass bowl over a saucepan. It is important that the bowl covers the top of the saucepan, and the bottom of the bowl must not touch the required one inch of water in the saucepan. You may want to acquire an "official" double boiler, which consists of two pans that are manufactured for a perfect fit (and most have a lid, to boot).

If chocolate is improperly melted (that is, too fast over too much heat), it may scorch and turn grainy. You can prevent this with a couple of precautions: do not heat the water so high that it simmers, and make certain that the bottom of the top half of the double boiler is not in contact with the water. My advice is to avoid distractions while melting chocolate.

Here is another caveat: a small amount of water in melted chocolate can ruin it. The process is called seizing, and it renders the chocolate texturally unusable. To avoid this unfortunate occurrence, be careful to wipe the moisture from the bottom of the top half of the double boiler before transferring chocolate from it to another container. Some folks suggest adding butter or vegetable oil to chocolate that has seized, but I do not agree. I have found that this remedy does not return the chocolate to its preferred silky, delicious state.

The good news is that high-quality chocolate seems to have some resilience, so if it gets a wee bit too hot or if a drop or two of water sneaks into the melted chocolate, it will probably be fine. Just remember that chocolate is a delightful ingredient to handle if a little tender loving care is used.

PORTIONING COOKIE DOUGH

You may notice in this book that the volume measure for cookie dough portions is usually given in tablespoons (sometimes heaping and sometimes not) and that the approximate weight of that tablespoon measure is parenthetically noted. You may also observe that at times the weight for a heaping tablespoon may vary as much as one-half ounce from one recipe to another. The reason for the weight variance depends on the density and content of the dough. The denser fruit- and nut-filled doughs will weigh more than others.

Although exact weights are important in measuring the ingredients for a dough, once the dough has been prepared, exact weights are not critical. So don't get overly obsessed about exact measurements when portioning the dough (the extra information is provided merely as a reference). The worst that can happen is that you will have bigger or smaller cookies (and therefore more or fewer in quantity), but there should be no harm done to the flavor.

SHIPPING COOKIES

As a young U.S. Marine in Vietnam, I always loved getting care packages from home, especially when they contained something made of chocolate. Considering what these packages went through to get from Woonsocket, Rhode Island, to Vietnam, it is amazing how well such items as homemade cookies and fudge fared. Less amazing is how quickly they were devoured. My favorite cookies, of course, were my mom's chocolate chip cookies (see Mrs. D's Chocolate Chip Cookies, page 43). Now that you have this recipe, you also can delight a loved one in a far-off locale with something special from your kitchen.

Many cookies have good shelf life and are perfect for shipping. A good general rule for shipping is to pack the cookies tightly in a sturdy container.

Pieces of wax paper or parchment paper layered between the cookies help prevent the cookies from arriving in crumbs (although that's not the end of the world). From personal experience, a package of confections from home means so much when you are in a far-away place.

SIFTING DRY INGREDIENTS

Many of our recipes call for sifting flour and other dry ingredients such as cocoa powder, baking powder, baking soda, and salt. Sifting helps ensure an even distribution of ingredients into a batter or dough. It also aerates these ingredients, which helps incorporate dry ingredients into wet ingredients. Additionally, it helps prevent the addition of foreign objects into a dough or batter.

Sifting dry ingredients onto a large piece of wax paper or parchment paper will keep your work area neat and it will also give you a vehicle to transport the sifted ingredients to the mixing bowl. Simply pull up the edges of the paper (that is why you need a large piece), and transfer the ingredients from countertop to mixing bowl.

STORING CONFECTIONS

Stored in a tightly sealed plastic container and held at room temperature, in the refrigerator, or in the freezer, many of the crunches, munches, and nibbles in this book can be stored for as long as several weeks. Each recipe in this book recommends an appropriate storage time and place. Additionally, I would suggest using wax paper in between layers of cookies that have been glazed, iced, or dusted.

TIMING AND INSTRUCTIONS

They say timing in life is crucial. It is also important in baking. But don't let the clock take the fun out of baking. If you are a novice, be prepared for some missteps. Usually this does not mean disaster, but mistakes can yield less-than-perfect results. Read through a recipe carefully and think of it as a road map. If you want to get from your kitchen to the land of crunchy cookies, munchy brownies, nibbles of chocolate, and slurps of ice cream, follow the directions to stay on the road, but don't be afraid to look at alternative routes.

EQUIPMENT

BAKING SHEETS

We have a collection of three dozen baking sheets at Ganache Hill. The majority are 10 x 15-inch nonstick sheets with sides, and we used these exclusively for testing recipes in this book. Baking sheets with sides are preferred because the sides help prevent the sheets from warping in the oven; this improved rigidity makes them easier and safer to handle.

If you have problems with hot spots in your oven (which translates into uneven baking), I suggest you investigate insulated baking sheets. These baking sheets have an insulating layer of air between two sheets of high-quality aluminum, resulting in evenly baked cookies even in the quirkiest of ovens. We discovered these baking sheets, marketed under the AirBake brand, just prior to moving into Ganache Hill, when we tested a few cookie recipes in my brand-new oven at home. Besides being 25 degrees Fahrenheit out of calibration, which we adjusted, the oven baked the cookies unevenly (even though we were switching the sheets on the racks and turning each one 180 degrees about halfway through the baking time). The AirBake sheets, which Jon Pierre found at a local discount department store, made perfect cookies every time.

The ovens at Ganache Hill distribute heat evenly and give us excellent results no matter what type of baking sheets we use, but it's good to know that there is a baking sheet available if you have an unreliable oven.

BOWLS

If you do not already own a set, consider purchasing a set of stainless steel bowls, preferably two or three of each size. We seem to use 1-, 3-, 4-, and 7-quart stainless steel bowls the most. Glass bowls have some of the same advantages as stainless steel bowls: they are easy to clean and noncorrosive, but they do shatter when dropped onto a ceramic tile floor. So for my money, stainless steel is the way to go.

COOLING RACK

See "Cooling Cookies" (page 9) for information on cooling racks.

DOUBLE BOILER

See "Melting Chocolate" (page 9) for information on double boilers.

ELECTRIC MIXER

A table-model (stand-up) electric mixer is, I believe, one of the more important pieces of equipment you can own if you are serious about baking. Most (but not all) of the doughs and batters in this book can be mixed by hand using a hand-held electric mixer, a whisk, a stiff rubber spatula, or even a wooden spoon (in which case you will have to use room-temperature butter), but only the table-model mixer has the strength to properly combine the ingredients in the densest doughs. It can also handle a larger volume of ingredients at one time than it is possible to mix by hand. If you are a smart cookie (I had to slip this in somewhere), you will invest in a table-model electric mixer.

FOOD PROCESSOR

As proud as I am of my skill with a knife, there are some tasks that cannot be done by hand as efficiently as with a food processor. Take the coconut in our recipe for Choco Cocos (see page 76), for instance. Here, twelve ounces of fresh coconut can be shredded in seconds using a food processor fitted with a shredding disk. If you try shredding it by hand either with a knife, a box grater, or with one of those gizmos they sell on the infomercials, it will take longer and the coconut will be neither as uniform nor as pretty. Of course shredding coconut is only one of the many tasks that a food processor does well. Try finely chopping two to three cups of nuts by hand versus processing them in seconds in a processor fitted with a metal blade. As they say, there's no contest.

ICE-CREAM FREEZER

Once you make your own ice cream, you will have found Xanadu. The difference in homemade versus store-bought (even the ice cream from those guys in Vermont) is dramatic.

If you are serious about getting into the ice-cream business, I suggest an electronically cooled countertop ice-cream freezer. This machine takes almost all the work out of the process and produces incredibly smooth ice creams and sorbets. For those who like to work for their pleasure, hand-cranked machines also produce dreamy results. They require a little elbow grease, but not like the machines of yore, which required constant cranking. The new machines do not require ice and salt to freeze the ingredients, either; rather, they have an insert called a freezing chamber that is removed from the machine and placed in the freezer for twelve hours or so prior to use. When you are ready to make the ice cream or sorbet, the freezing chamber is removed from the freezer and inserted back into the machine; from then on, it requires only the occasional crank. One drawback, however, is that many of these machines make only one quart of ice cream or less. Look for a machine that will produce one and one-half to two quarts. After all, if you're going to hand-crank, the reward should be substantial.

ICE-WATER BATH

Just about everyone has the equipment required to fashion this necessary tool, which can be as simple as a sink filled with ice water. You may also fashion an ice-water bath using two different-sized bowls: a 7-quart bowl could hold the ice water and then a 3- or 4-quart bowl could hold the ingredients to be chilled. First, a container holding the ingredients to be cooled is placed in the ice water (if the container floats you have too much water). Then the ingredients should be stirred frequently for efficient and quick cooling. This fast cooling serves a couple of important purposes: it inhibits the growth of bacteria, so the food is less likely to spoil, and it also helps you complete the recipe more quickly.

OVENS

See "Ovens" (page 7) for information on ovens.

RUBBER SPATULA

With a rubber spatula you can remove all of the melted chocolate, ganache, dough, or whatever else you are trying to transfer from one container to another. Additionally, it is the tool that most effectively finishes mixing a dough or batter until it is thoroughly combined.

If you are like me you probably have a few spatulas that have been subjected to various stages of meltdown. Recently a new heat-resistant rubber spatula has hit the marketplace. Sold as a "high-heat spatula," it is great for working with very hot ingredients.

SERRATED KNIFE WITH ROUNDED TIP

With this knife you will be able to cut brownies and bar cookies while they are still in the pan without destroying the nonstick coating.

THERMOMETERS

Oven Thermometer

Under "Ovens" (page 7), I mention the importance of having an accurate gauge of the heat produced by your oven. The most reliable way of knowing your oven temperature is to use an oven thermometer. I recommend mercury-filled tube thermometers, which are more precise (and slightly more expensive) than the spring-style thermometers. The mercury thermometer may be left in the oven at all times, except when you electronically clean your oven, a process that will ruin the thermometer.

Instant-Read Test Thermometers

Not designed for oven use, an instant-read test thermometer with a range of 0–200 degrees Fahrenheit is needed for the ice-cream recipes in this book. For the Pumpkin Pecan Chocolate Chunk Fritters (see page 102), you will need an instant-read test thermometer with a range of 50–550 degrees Fahrenheit.

Easy Street

OPPOSITE: **Chocolate Crackups (see page 18)**   ABOVE: **Chocolate Jungle Crunch (see page 33)**

CHOCOLATE DALMATIANS
Yields 4 dozen 2-inch cookies

INGREDIENTS

4 ounces white chocolate, chopped into ¼-inch pieces

¾ pound unsalted butter, cut into 1-ounce pieces

1 cup granulated sugar

2 teaspoons pure vanilla extract

4 cups all-purpose flour

½ teaspoon salt

8 ounces semisweet chocolate mini-morsels

EQUIPMENT

Cook's knife, cutting board, measuring cups, measuring spoons, double boiler, rubber spatula, 1-quart bowl, table-model electric mixer with paddle, wax paper, 4 nonstick baking sheets, plastic cookie storage container with lid

THE CHEF'S TOUCH

How many chocolate mini-morsels are in this recipe? If you said 3,168, you're exactly right. Any fewer just wouldn't be enough!

See "Notes from Ganache Hill" (page 6) for purchasing information on white chocolate.

Because this is a very stiff dough, you'll need to use a table-model mixer to properly mix the dough.

Chocolate Dalmatians will keep for several days at room temperature if stored in a tightly sealed plastic container. For long-term storage, up to several weeks, the cookies may be frozen. Freeze the cookies in a tightly sealed plastic container to prevent dehydration and protect them from freezer odors.

MAKE THE DALMATIANS

Preheat the oven to 325 degrees Fahrenheit.

Heat 1 inch of water in the bottom half of a double boiler over medium heat. With the heat on, place the white chocolate in the top half of the double boiler. Use a rubber spatula to stir the chocolate until completely melted and smooth, about 2 minutes. Transfer the melted chocolate to a 1-quart bowl and set aside until needed.

Place the butter and sugar in the bowl of an electric mixer fitted with a paddle. Beat on medium for 4 minutes until soft. Use a rubber spatula to scrape down the sides of the bowl, then beat on high for 4 more minutes until light (but not fluffy). Add the vanilla extract and the melted white chocolate. Beat on medium for 1 minute. Operate the mixer on low while gradually adding the flour and salt; mix for 1 minute. Scrape down the sides of the bowl. Add the chocolate mini-morsels and mix on low for 30 seconds. Remove the bowl from the mixer and use a rubber spatula to finish mixing the ingredients until thoroughly combined.

Portion the dough into 48 slightly heaping tablespoon-size pieces (approximately 1 ounce per piece) onto a large piece of wax paper. Gently roll each portion in the palms of your hands to form a ball (this is not a sticky dough, so you should not need to dampen your hands as recommended in other recipes). Divide the dough balls onto 4 nonstick baking sheets, 12 evenly spaced balls per sheet. Place the baking sheets on the top and center racks of the preheated oven and bake for 14 to 16 minutes, rotating the sheets from top to center halfway through the baking time (at that time also turn each sheet 180 degrees). Remove the cookies from the oven and cool to room temperature on the baking sheets, about 20 minutes. Store the cooled cookies in a tightly sealed plastic container.

CHOCOLATE QUICKIES

Yields 3 dozen 2½-inch cookies

INGREDIENTS

2 cups all-purpose flour

½ cup unsweetened cocoa powder

1 teaspoon baking powder

1 teaspoon salt

½ pound unsalted butter, cut into
   1-ounce pieces

1 cup granulated sugar

3 large eggs

1 tablespoon pure vanilla extract

2 cups semisweet chocolate chips

EQUIPMENT

Measuring cups, measuring spoons, cook's knife, cutting board, sifter, wax paper, table-model electric mixer with paddle, rubber spatula, 3 nonstick baking sheets, plastic cookie storage container with lid

THE CHEF'S TOUCH

From start to finish, Chocolate Quickies take about 30 minutes to make, and though they are delicious warm, for the sake of your tongue you should let them cool down a bit. Not surprisingly, Quickies are often gone before you know it.

Chocolate Quickies will keep for several days at room temperature in a tightly sealed plastic container. They will also keep for more than a week covered with plastic wrap in the refrigerator. For long-term storage, up to several weeks, these cookies may be frozen. Freeze the quickies in a tightly sealed plastic container to prevent dehydration and to protect them from freezer odors.

MAKE THE QUICKIES

Preheat the oven to 350 degrees Fahrenheit.

In a sifter combine the flour, cocoa powder, baking powder, and salt. Sift onto a large piece of wax paper and set aside until needed.

Place the butter and sugar in the bowl of an electric mixer fitted with a paddle. Beat on medium for 3 minutes until soft. Use a rubber spatula to scrape down the sides of the bowl, then add the eggs and vanilla extract and beat on medium for 2 minutes until smooth. Scrape down the bowl. Beat on high for 3 minutes until very smooth. Scrape down the bowl once more. Operate the mixer on low while gradually adding the sifted dry ingredients until incorporated, about 30 seconds. Add the chocolate chips and mix on low for 30 seconds longer until incorporated. Remove the bowl from the mixer and use a rubber spatula to finish mixing the dough until thoroughly combined.

Using a heaping tablespoon of dough for each cookie (approximately 1¼ ounces), portion 12 cookies, evenly spaced, onto each of 3 nonstick baking sheets. Use your fingers to slightly flatten each portion of dough. Place the baking sheets on the top and center racks of the preheated oven and bake for 10 to 12 minutes (no need to rotate the sheets). Remove the cookies from the oven and cool to room temperature on the baking sheets, about 30 minutes. Store the cooled cookies in a tightly sealed plastic container.

COCOA ALMOND SHORTIES

Yields 4 dozen 2¾-inch cookies

INGREDIENTS

1¼ cups sliced almonds
1   pound unsalted butter, cut into
    1-ounce pieces
1½ cups granulated sugar
5   level tablespoons unsweetened
    cocoa powder
2   tablespoons dark crème de cacao
4   cups all-purpose flour
½   teaspoon salt

EQUIPMENT

Measuring cups, cook's knife, cutting board, measuring spoons, 4 nonstick baking sheets, food processor with metal blade, table-model electric mixer with paddle, rubber spatula, wax paper, dinner fork, sifter, plastic cookie storage container with lid

THE CHEF'S TOUCH

Cocoa Almond Shorties are long on flavor. An ideal complement of butter, cocoa, and almonds makes them predictably delicious; the touch of crème de cacao adds a surprise; and they're quick and easy to make.

Since this dough is very stiff, I do not recommend mixing it with any piece of equipment other than a table-model electric mixer.

Cocoa Almond Shorties will keep for several days at room temperature if stored in a tightly sealed plastic container. For long-term storage, up to several weeks, the Shorties may be frozen before they have been dusted with cocoa powder (bring the frozen cookies to room temperature before dusting). Freeze the Shorties in a tightly sealed plastic container to prevent dehydration and to protect them from freezer odors.

MAKE THE SHORTIES

Preheat the oven to 325 degrees Fahrenheit.

Toast the almonds in the preheated oven until golden brown, about 10 to 12 minutes. Cool the nuts to room temperature before finely chopping in a food processor with a metal blade (the nuts may also be chopped by hand using a cook's knife).

Place the butter and sugar in the bowl of an electric mixer fitted with a paddle. Beat on medium for 2 minutes until soft. Use a rubber spatula to scrape down the sides of the bowl, then beat on high for 3 minutes until the batter is light (but not fluffy). Add 4 tablespoons cocoa powder and the dark crème de cacao. Beat on medium for 30 seconds. Operate the mixer on low while adding the flour, almonds, and salt, and mix for 1 minute until incorporated. Remove the bowl from the mixer and use a rubber spatula to finish mixing the dough until thoroughly combined.

Divide the dough into 48 slightly heaping tablespoon–size pieces (approximately 1 ounce per piece) onto a large piece of wax paper. Gently roll each portion in the palms of your hands to form a ball. Divide the dough balls onto 4 nonstick baking sheets, 12 evenly spaced balls per sheet. Use the back of a fork to press each ball into a disk that is 2 inches in diameter and ½ inch thick. Place the baking sheets on the top and center racks of the preheated oven and bake for 10 to 12 minutes, rotating the sheets from top to center halfway through the baking time (at that time also turn each sheet 180 degrees). Remove the cookies from the oven and cool to room temperature on the baking sheets, about 20 minutes. Use a sifter to uniformly dust the tops of the cookies with the remaining unsweetened cocoa powder. Store the cooled cookies in a tightly sealed plastic container.

VERY "RICH" CHOCOLATE CHERRY WALNUT BARS

Yields 4 dozen 1-inch bars

MAKE IT "RICH"

Preheat the oven to 325 degrees Fahrenheit.

Toast the walnuts on a baking sheet with sides in the preheated oven until lightly golden brown, about 10 minutes. Remove the walnuts from the oven and cool to room temperature.

Place 2 cups toasted walnuts and ¼ cup granulated sugar in the bowl of a food processor fitted with a metal blade. Process until finely chopped, about 2 minutes. Transfer the nut mixture to the 9×13×2-inch nonstick baking pan. Use your fingertips to press the mixture onto the bottom of the pan and into the corners and sides, creating an even layer. Set aside.

Heat the dried cherries and cherry juice in a 3-quart saucepan over medium-high heat. Bring to a boil, then remove from the heat and allow to cool at room temperature for 30 minutes.

Sprinkle the cooled cherry-and-juice mixture evenly over the walnut mixture in the pan in an even layer. Set aside.

Heat the brown sugar and heavy cream in a 5-quart saucepan over medium-high heat. Bring to a boil, stirring occasionally to dissolve the sugar. Adjust the heat and allow the mixture to simmer for 15 minutes. Remove from the heat and stir in the chocolate. Transfer the mixture to a 5-quart bowl. Add the butter and stir to combine. Add the remaining cup walnuts, stirring to combine. Pour the chocolate mixture (this is a lovely sight) into the baking pan and spread over the cherry mixture in an even layer. Refrigerate for 2 hours before cutting.

Use a serrated knife with a rounded tip to cut the Very "Rich" Chocolate Cherry Walnut Bar into 24 2-inch squares, then cut each square in half to make 48 bars. For a clean cut, heat the blade of the knife under hot running water and wipe the blade dry before making each cut. Allow the bars to stand at room temperature for 30 minutes before serving. Serve the bars immediately or refrigerate in a tightly sealed plastic container.

INGREDIENTS

- **3** cups walnut pieces
- **¼** cup granulated sugar
- **3** cups dried cherries
- **½** cup 100% natural unsweetened cherry juice
- **2** cups light brown sugar
- **1** cup heavy cream
- **2** ounces unsweetened chocolate, chopped into ¼-inch pieces
- **6** tablespoons unsalted butter at room temperature

EQUIPMENT

Measuring cups, baking sheet with sides, measuring spoons, cook's knife, cutting board, food processor with metal blade, 9×13×2-inch nonstick rectangular baking pan, 3-quart saucepan, 5-quart bowl, serrated knife with rounded tip, plastic container with lid

THE CHEF'S TOUCH

Be forewarned: while you don't have to be as rich as a rajah to prepare this recipe, it wouldn't hurt. Dried cherries (particularly three cups of them) are pretty expensive. But you'll know it's worth every penny after the first bite.

Very "Rich" Chocolate Cherry Walnut Bars will keep for several days if stored in a tightly sealed plastic container in the refrigerator. The bars are best when served cold from the refrigerator with a glass of milk. Or send the kids to bed and serve the bars with a favorite postprandial beverage and explore just how rich life can be.

CHOCOLATE CRACKUPS

Yields 3 dozen 2½-inch cookies

THE CHEF'S TOUCH

I find the transformation from sugar-coated ball to Chocolate Crackup Cookie a rather cosmic experience. If your oven has a window, turn on the light and take a peek: first the ball of dough collapses into a 2½-inch disk, and then as the cookies bake, the confectioners' sugar–coated surface begins to "crack up." As the fissures begin erupting, the cookie takes on its distinctive look. You say you have better things to do than watch cookies morph? Well, just don't forget to rotate and turn the pans halfway through the baking time—of course, by then you will have missed the show.

I note in the recipe to evenly and generously coat the dough balls with the confectioners' sugar. The effect of the cookie is enhanced by the generosity of the sugar; a light dusting of sugar would create a much less dramatic cookie.

Chocolate Crackups will keep for several days at room temperature if stored in a tightly sealed plastic container. For long-term storage, up to several weeks, the cookie may be frozen. Freeze the Crackups in a tightly sealed plastic container to prevent dehydration and to protect them from freezer odors.

Note: Photograph appears on page 12.

INGREDIENTS

- **4** ounces unsweetened chocolate, chopped into ¼-inch pieces
- **2** cups granulated sugar
- **½** cup vegetable oil
- **4** large eggs
- **2** teaspoons pure vanilla extract
- **2** cups all-purpose flour
- **1½** teaspoons baking powder
- **½** teaspoon salt
- **1** cup confectioners' sugar

EQUIPMENT

Cook's knife, cutting board, measuring cups, measuring spoons, double boiler, rubber spatula, 1-quart bowl, 7-quart bowl, stiff whisk, plastic wrap, wax paper, 3 nonstick baking sheets, plastic cookie storage container with lid

MAKE THE CHOCOLATE CRACKUPS

Heat 1 inch of water in the bottom half of a double boiler over medium heat. With the heat on, place the unsweetened chocolate in the top half of the double boiler. Use a rubber spatula to stir the chocolate until completely melted and smooth, about 3 minutes. Transfer the melted chocolate to a 1-quart bowl and set aside until needed.

Combine the granulated sugar and vegetable oil in a 7-quart bowl, using a stiff whisk to stir until the sugar resembles wet (white) sand. Add the eggs and vanilla extract and whisk vigorously until incorporated. Add the melted chocolate and stir until silky. Add the flour, baking powder, and salt, and blend with a rubber spatula until smooth. Tightly cover the bowl with plastic wrap and refrigerate for 1 hour.

Preheat the oven to 350 degrees Fahrenheit.

Remove the dough from the refrigerator and discard the plastic wrap. Divide the cookie dough into 36 slightly heaping tablespoon-size pieces (approximately 1 ounce per piece) onto a large piece of wax paper. Place the confectioners' sugar in a 1-quart bowl. Gently roll each portion in the palms of your hands to form a smooth ball (keep a towel close by since it gets a little sticky between the first and the thirty-sixth ball). Then roll each ball in the confectioners' sugar to coat evenly and generously.

Divide the balls onto 3 nonstick baking sheets, 12 evenly spaced balls per sheet (they expand so don't crowd). Place the baking sheets on the top and center racks of the preheated oven and bake for 12 to 14 minutes, rotating the sheets from top to center halfway through the baking time (at that time also turn each sheet 180 degrees). Remove the cookies from the oven and cool to room temperature on the baking sheets, about 30 minutes. Store the cooled cookies in a tightly sealed plastic container until ready to serve.

CHOCOLATE PEANUT BUTTER LOVE BARS
Yields 4 dozen 1-inch bars

BELLY UP TO THE BARS

Preheat the oven to 350 degrees Fahrenheit.

Toast the peanuts on a baking sheet in the preheated oven until golden brown, about 8 to 10 minutes. Cool the nuts to room temperature before chopping by hand with a cook's knife into ¼-inch pieces.

Use a stiff whisk to blend together the peanut butter and brown sugar in a 7-quart bowl. Add the eggs and vanilla extract and whisk until thoroughly blended. Add the peanuts and the chopped semisweet chocolate and use a rubber spatula to mix together until thoroughly combined. Transfer the mixture to the 9×13×2-inch nonstick baking pan. Use your fingertips to press the mixture onto the bottom of the pan and into the corners and sides, creating an even layer. Place the pan on the center rack of the preheated oven and bake for 22 minutes until set in the center. Remove from the oven and cool at room temperature for 1 hour before cutting.

Use a serrated knife with rounded tip to cut the Chocolate Peanut Butter Love Bar into 24 2-inch squares, then cut each square in half to make 48 bars. For clean edges, heat the blade of the knife under hot running water and wipe the blade dry before making each cut. Serve immediately or store the bars in a tightly sealed plastic container.

INGREDIENTS

- **2** cups unsalted peanuts
- **2** cups creamy peanut butter
- **2** cups tightly packed light brown sugar
- **2** large eggs
- **1** teaspoon pure vanilla extract
- **1** pound semisweet chocolate, chopped into ¼-inch pieces

EQUIPMENT

Measuring cups, measuring spoons, cook's knife, cutting board, baking sheet, stiff whisk, 7-quart bowl, rubber spatula, 9×13×2-inch nonstick rectangular baking pan, serrated knife with rounded tip, plastic cookie storage container with lid

THE CHEF'S TOUCH

I love peanuts. Peanuts are one of my vices. The only thing better than peanuts is peanuts with chocolate. Add peanut butter to that, and the only thing missing from this picture of Nirvana is my soulmate and a South Pacific setting. But I digress....

This batter is pretty sticky, so you'll need a rubber spatula to remove batter stuck between the strands of the whisk during the mixing.

Chocolate Peanut Butter Love Bars will keep for a week or so at room temperature in a tightly sealed plastic container. Truth is, these bars are nearly indestructible, so if you are planning a cozy ocean crossing for two, be certain to stock up.

CHOCOLATE CHUNK "MACAROONIES"

Yields 4 dozen 2-inch cookies

THE CHEF'S TOUCH

Almond paste gives classic macaroons their distinctive flavor, and the addition of coconut makes the popular cookie even better. Our Macaroonie was inspired by this classic paradigm; however, replacing the almond paste with chopped almonds lightens the texture and the flavor, and the touch of cream cheese makes the Macaroonies dissolve in your mouth like a whiff of perfume in the breeze. Although I like classic macaroons, I love these tiny, chocolate-flecked neoclassics.

You'll notice that this recipe and this book contain no sweetened flaked coconut, which tastes less like coconut and more like the sugar, preservatives, and whiteners that render it gummy and bland. Instead, we use frozen coconut, which is widely available and delivers both the flavor and texture we all love in coconut. (We actually tried using fresh coconut for this recipe, but the results were not remarkably better and did not justify the amount of extra work involved.) Make sure you thoroughly drain the frozen coconut before using, or you will be disappointed with the results. Look for frozen coconut in your grocer's frozen baked goods section.

Chocolate Chunk Macaroonies will keep for several days at room temperature if stored in a tightly sealed plastic container. The texture of the cookie is adversely affected by refrigeration and freezing.

Offering a platter of Macaroonies along with hot coffee would be a charming way to bring an evening of food and friends to a close, but then they may never want to leave.

INGREDIENTS

2 cups sliced almonds
6 ounces frozen grated coconut, thawed
1¼ cups all-purpose flour
1 tablespoon baking powder
¼ teaspoon salt
¼ pound unsalted butter at room temperature
⅔ cup granulated sugar
2 ounces cream cheese at room temperature
2 large egg yolks
1 teaspoon pure vanilla extract
4 ounces semisweet chocolate, chopped into ¼-inch pieces

EQUIPMENT

Measuring cups, measuring spoons, cook's knife, cutting board, 4 nonstick baking sheets, 4-quart bowl, medium-gauge strainer, rubber spatula, sifter, wax paper, 7-quart bowl, plastic cookie storage container with lid

MAKE THE CHOCOLATE CHUNK MACAROONIES

Preheat the oven to 350 degrees Fahrenheit.

Toast the almonds on a baking sheet in the preheated oven for 8 minutes. Cool them to room temperature, then place the sliced almonds in a 4-quart bowl and use your hands to break them into irregular pieces. Set aside until needed.

Place the thawed coconut in a medium-gauge strainer. Using a rubber spatula, press down on the coconut to drain the excess moisture from the coconut (discard the liquid). Set aside.

In a sifter combine the flour, baking powder, and salt. Sift onto a large piece of wax paper and set aside until needed.

In a 7-quart bowl, cream the butter, sugar, and cream cheese with a stiff rubber spatula (or a wooden spoon) until smooth. Combine the egg yolks and vanilla extract into this mix. Add the coconut and mix until thoroughly combined. Now add the sifted dry ingredients and continue mixing until fully incorporated. Finally, mix in the chopped chocolate.

Divide the cookie dough into 48 level tablespoon–size pieces (approximately ½ ounce per cookie) onto a large sheet of wax paper. Individually roll each dough portion in the almonds to coat thoroughly (use your hands to form the almonds around each portion). Place the portions on 4 nonstick baking sheets, 12 evenly spaced portions per baking sheet. Place the baking sheets on the top and center racks of the preheated oven and bake for 12 minutes, until lightly golden brown around the edges. Rotate the sheets from top to center and turn each sheet 180 degrees about halfway through the baking time. Remove the Macaroonies from the oven and allow to cool at room temperature for 30 minutes. Store the Macaroonies in a tightly sealed plastic container until ready to serve.

WALNUT TOFFEE TRIANGLES
Yields 4 dozen 1-inch triangles

1 cup toasted walnuts

½ pound unsalted butter at room temperature

1¼ cups tightly packed dark brown sugar

2 large egg yolks

1 teaspoon pure vanilla extract

2¼ cups all-purpose flour

½ teaspoon salt

1 pound semisweet chocolate, chopped into ¼-inch pieces

EQUIPMENT

Measuring cups, measuring spoons, cook's knife, cutting board, baking sheet, food processor with metal blade, 7-quart bowl, rubber spatula, 9×13×2-inch nonstick rectangular baking pan, cake spatula, serrated knife with rounded tip, plastic cookie storage container with lid

THE CHEF'S TOUCH

This is an atypical toffee recipe because the result is neither hard nor brittle. But don't intellectualize it—just enjoy it (and give your dentist a break).

Walnut Toffee Triangles will keep for 2 to 3 days at room temperature if stored in a tightly sealed plastic container. For longer storage, up to a week, the Triangles may be covered with plastic wrap and refrigerated. For long-term storage, up to several weeks, the Triangles may be frozen. Freeze the Triangles in a tightly sealed plastic container to prevent dehydration and to protect them from freezer odors.

MAKE THE TRIANGLES

Preheat the oven to 350 degrees Fahrenheit.

Toast the walnuts on a baking sheet in the preheated oven for 6 minutes. Cool the nuts to room temperature.

Process the walnuts in a food processor fitted with a metal blade until finely chopped, about 8 to 10 seconds. Set aside until needed.

Place the butter and sugar in a 7-quart bowl. Use a rubber spatula to mix the ingredients together until well blended. Add the egg yolks and vanilla extract and combine until incorporated. Add the flour and salt and blend together until the mixture is smooth and thoroughly combined. Transfer the mixture to the 9×13×2-inch nonstick baking pan. Use your fingertips to press the mixture (the dough is not sticky) onto the bottom of the pan and into the corners and sides, creating an even layer. Place the pan on the center rack of the preheated oven and bake for 20 minutes, until light golden brown. Remove it from the oven and immediately sprinkle the chopped semisweet chocolate over the hot toffee. Allow to stand for 5 minutes. Use a cake spatula to spread the melted chocolate in a silky smooth and even layer. Sprinkle the chopped walnuts over the melted chocolate in an even layer. Allow to cool to room temperature for 30 minutes before cutting.

Use a serrated knife with rounded tip to cut the Walnut Toffee into 24 2-inch squares, then cut each square in half diagonally to form triangles. For a clean cut, heat the blade of the knife under hot running water and wipe the blade dry before making each cut. Serve immediately or store in a tightly sealed plastic container.

ALMIGHTY CHOCOLATE DIVINITY

Yields 2 dozen 2-inch bites

INGREDIENTS

3 cups granulated sugar

½ cup water

⅓ cup light corn syrup

2 large egg whites

1 cup finely chopped toasted walnuts

8 ounces semisweet chocolate mini-morsels

CREATE THE DIVINITY

Heat the granulated sugar, water, and corn syrup in a 3-quart saucepan over medium-high heat, stirring to dissolve the sugar. Bring to a boil. Continue to boil, stirring often, until the temperature of the syrup reaches 250 degrees Fahrenheit, about 5 minutes.

As soon as the syrup begins boiling, place the egg whites in the bowl of an electric mixer fitted with a balloon whip. Whisk on high until soft peaks form, about 4 minutes. Change the mixer speed to medium. Carefully and slowly pour the 250-degree-Fahrenheit syrup into the whisked egg whites, and continue to whisk on medium until the meringue is very thick, about 4 minutes. Remove the bowl from the mixer. Working quickly, use a rubber spatula to fold the walnuts and then the chocolate morsels into the meringue, creating a variegated mixture. Divide the mixture into 24 heaping tablespoons onto two large pieces of wax paper, using your finger to push the mixture off the spoon and onto the wax paper. Allow to cool to room temperature for about an hour before storing in a tightly sealed plastic container.

EQUIPMENT

Measuring cups, baking sheet, food processor with metal blade, 3-quart saucepan, whisk, instant-read test thermometer, table-model electric mixer with balloon whip, rubber spatula, measuring spoons, wax paper, plastic cookie storage container with lid

THE CHEF'S TOUCH

For the ultimate texture and flavor for the Almighty Chocolate Divinity, be sure to toast the walnuts in a 350-degree-Fahrenheit oven for 5 to 6 minutes. Don't chop the nuts until they have cooled to room temperature. A food processor fitted with a metal blade will finely chop the nuts in just a few seconds, or you can use a cook's knife to chop the nuts.

Practice makes perfect with this lovely, cloudlike candy. If your Divinity looks less like a cumulus and more like a downpour, don't despair; it will still be quite tasty.

Almighty Chocolate Divinity will keep for 2 to 3 days at room temperature if stored in a tightly sealed plastic container. The Divinity will keep for a few more days under refrigeration (I actually prefer this candy chilled). For long-term storage, up to several weeks, the candy may be frozen in a tightly sealed plastic container to prevent dehydration and to protect it from freezer odors.

BROWN SUGAR CHOCOLATE CHIP BARS

Yields 4 dozen 1-inch bars

INGREDIENTS

1¾ cups all-purpose flour

1   teaspoon baking soda

½   teaspoon salt

1½ cups tightly packed light brown
    sugar

½   pound unsalted butter at room
    temperature

½   cup granulated sugar

2   large eggs

1   teaspoon pure vanilla extract

1   cup semisweet chocolate chips

EQUIPMENT

Measuring cups, measuring spoons, sifter, wax paper, 7-quart bowl, stiff rubber spatula or wooden spoon, 9×13×2-inch nonstick rectangular baking pan, serrated knife with rounded tip, plastic cookie storage container with lid

THE CHEF'S TOUCH

When is enough in fact enough? Around our house the answer is "never." Trellis pastry chef Kelly Bailey came up with these over-the-top bar cookies to assuage my voracious sweet tooth, delivering the finest example of out-of-control confection that I have had in some time. Tie me down, but don't take away my Brown Sugar Chocolate Chip Bars.

Brown Sugar Chocolate Chip Bars will keep for several days or more at room temperature in a tightly sealed plastic container. The bars taste best at room temperature with a glass of skim milk on the side.

MAKE THE BROWN SUGAR CHOCOLATE CHIP BARS

Preheat the oven to 325 degrees Fahrenheit.

In a sifter combine the flour, baking soda, and salt. Sift onto a large piece of wax paper and set aside until needed.

Place the brown sugar, butter, and granulated sugar in a 7-quart bowl. Use a stiff rubber spatula or a wooden spoon to cream the sugar and butter together until very smooth. Add the eggs and combine until incorporated. Add the vanilla extract and combine until incorporated. Add the sifted dry ingredients, followed by the chocolate chips. Combine until thoroughly incorporated.

Transfer the batter to the nonstick baking pan, using a rubber spatula to spread the batter in an even layer. Bake on the center rack of the preheated oven for 40 minutes until uniformly golden brown. Remove the pan from the oven and allow to cool at room temperature for 1 hour before cutting

Use a serrated knife with rounded tip to cut the Brown Sugar Chocolate Chip Bar into 24 2-inch squares, then cut the squares in half to make 48 bars. For a clean cut, heat the blade of the knife under hot running water and wipe the blade dry before making each cut. Serve immediately or store in a tightly sealed plastic container.

CHOCOLATE RASPBERRY "COOKIECUPCAKES"

Makes 3 dozen mini-cupcakes

INGREDIENTS

1	cup all-purpose flour
1	teaspoon baking soda
¼	teaspoon salt
¾	cup heavy cream
4	ounces unsweetened chocolate, chopped into ¼-inch pieces
2	large eggs
½	cup granulated sugar
1	teaspoon pure vanilla extract
8	ounces semisweet chocolate mini-morsels
1	cup fresh red raspberries

EQUIPMENT

Measuring cups, measuring spoons, cook's knife, cutting board, sifter, wax paper, double boiler, rubber spatula, 1-quart bowl, electric mixer with paddle, 3 nonstick 12-cup miniature muffin tins, toothpick, plastic cookie storage container with lid

CREATE THE COOKIECUPCAKES

Preheat the oven to 375 degrees Fahrenheit.

In a sifter combine the flour, baking soda, and salt. Sift onto a large piece of wax paper and set aside until needed.

Heat 1 inch of water in the bottom half of a double boiler over medium heat. With the heat on, place the heavy cream and the unsweetened chocolate in the top half of the double boiler. Use a rubber spatula to stir the mixture until completely melted and smooth, about 5 to 6 minutes. Transfer the melted chocolate-and-cream mixture to a 1-quart bowl and set aside until needed.

Place the eggs, granulated sugar, and vanilla extract in the bowl of an electric mixer fitted with a paddle. Beat on medium for 2 minutes. Use a rubber spatula to scrape down the sides of the bowl, then continue to beat on medium for 2 more minutes. Scrape down the bowl. Add the melted chocolate-and-cream mixture and beat on medium for 1 minute. Operate the mixer on low while gradually adding the sifted dry ingredients; mix for 1 minute. Remove the bowl from the mixer and add the chocolate mini-morsels and the raspberries. Use a rubber spatula to fold the batter together until thoroughly combined (although this batter looks good enough to eat, the raw eggs make it unwise to do so).

Put one heaping tablespoonful of batter into each of the 36 miniature muffin cups. Place the muffin tins on the top and center racks of the preheated oven and bake until a toothpick inserted in the center of a cupcake comes out clean, about 10 minutes. Rotate the tins from top to center halfway through the baking time, and also turn each tin 180 degrees. Remove the cupcakes from the oven and allow to cool at room temperature for 15 minutes. Store the cupcakes in a tightly sealed plastic container until ready to serve.

THE CHEF'S TOUCH

If you don't have unsweetened chocolate, you may substitute semisweet chocolate, which will yield a slightly sweeter Cookiecupcake.

Thanks to agricultural countries south of the Equator, fresh red raspberries are now available year-round (Chilean raspberries are delicious and not terribly expensive). I do not recommend frozen raspberries for this recipe, since their near-liquefied state will alter the texture and flavor of the Cookiecupcakes.

Chocolate Raspberry Cookiecupcakes will keep for a couple of days at room temperature in a tightly sealed plastic container (longer than that and your minis will become moldies), or covered with plastic wrap in the refrigerator. For long-term storage, up to several weeks, these cupcakes may be frozen. Freeze the Cookiecupcakes in a tightly sealed plastic container to prevent dehydration and to protect them from freezer odors. Thaw the cupcakes at room temperature for 1 hour before serving.

CHOCOLATE CASHEW COCONUT CLUSTERS

Yields 2 dozen 2-inch clusters

INGREDIENTS

2 cups unsalted cashews

8 ounces shredded dried coconut

1 pound semisweet chocolate, chopped into ¼-inch pieces

EQUIPMENT

Measuring cups, cook's knife, cutting board, baking sheet, double boiler, rubber spatula, 4-quart bowl, measuring spoons, wax paper, plastic cookie storage container with lid

THE CHEF'S TOUCH

More candy than cookie, a Chocolate Cashew Coconut Cluster won't break a healthy tooth, but it could break the bank. They are expensive, consisting of nothing but the finest chocolate, cashews, and coconut. These clusters are a very direct hit of chocolate—no butter, no cream—so I recommend splurging on the highest quality chocolate you can purchase in order to yield the most exquisite clusters.

Look for dried coconut flakes in the bulk food (dried fruit, nuts, dried beans, and so on) section at your specialty grocer or major supermarket.

After the Clusters are firm enough to handle, store them in a tightly sealed plastic container in the refrigerator for up to several days until ready to enjoy. Unfortunately, these Clusters were not made for traveling, so eat them up at home (serve them in paper candy cups).

MAKE THE CHOCOLATE CASHEW COCONUT CLUSTERS

Preheat the oven to 325 degrees Fahrenheit.

Toast the cashews on a baking sheet in the preheated oven for 20 minutes until uniformly golden brown. Cool the nuts to room temperature.

Toast the coconut on a baking sheet in the preheated oven until lightly golden around the edges, about 10 minutes. Cool the coconut to room temperature.

Heat 1 inch of water in the bottom half of a double boiler over medium heat. With the heat on, place the semisweet chocolate in the top half of the double boiler. Use a rubber spatula to stir the chocolate until completely melted and smooth, about 5 to 6 minutes. Transfer the melted chocolate to a 4-quart bowl. Add the cashews and coconut. Use a rubber spatula to stir the mixture until the cashews and coconut are completely coated with chocolate.

Immediately portion 24 clusters, 1 heaping tablespoon (approximately 1½ ounces) of mixture per cluster, onto wax paper. Allow the clusters to harden at room temperature for 1 hour, then refrigerate for 30 minutes until firm enough to handle. Store the clusters in a tightly sealed plastic container in the refrigerator until ready to serve.

CHOCOLATE DROP SHORTCAKES

Yields 2 dozen 2½-inch biscuits

MAKE THE CHOCOLATE DROP SHORTCAKES

Preheat the oven to 400 degrees Fahrenheit.

Heat the milk and the granulated sugar in a 1½-quart saucepan over medium-high heat. When hot, stir to dissolve the sugar. Bring to a boil. Immediately remove from the heat and transfer to a 4-quart bowl. Cool in an ice-water bath to a temperature of 40 to 45 degrees Fahrenheit. Cover with plastic wrap and refrigerate until needed.

In a sifter combine the flour, cocoa powder, baking powder, and salt. Sift into a 7-quart bowl. Add the butter. Use a fork to "cut" the butter into the sifted flour mixture until the mixture develops a mealy texture. Add the chocolate mini-morsels and use a rubber spatula to mix until combined. Add the chilled milk mixture and mix with the spatula until the dough comes together.

Using a heaping tablespoon of dough (approximately 1½ounces) per shortcake, portion 12 shortcakes, evenly spaced, onto each of 2 nonstick baking sheets. Place the baking sheets on the center rack of the preheated oven and bake for 12 minutes. Remove the shortcakes from the oven and cool at room temperature for 10 minutes. Serve the warm shortcakes immediately, or cool completely and store in a tightly sealed plastic container.

INGREDIENTS

1	cup whole milk
¼	cup granulated sugar
1¾	cups all-purpose flour
½	cup unsweetened cocoa powder
2	tablespoons baking powder
1	teaspoon salt
8	tablespoons unsalted butter, chilled
8	ounces semisweet chocolate mini-morsels

EQUIPMENT

Measuring cups, measuring spoons, 1½-quart saucepan, 4-quart bowl, instant-read test thermometer, plastic wrap, sifter, 7-quart bowl, fork, rubber spatula, 2 nonstick baking sheets, plastic cookie storage container with lid

THE CHEF'S TOUCH

My mother loved serving our family strawberry shortcake after dinner on Sundays in the summer. Although hers wasn't chocolate, we loved it anyway (my siblings share my passion for chocolate). It is probably a good thing she didn't have this chocolate shortcake recipe—she may never have gotten rid of us.

Chocolate Drop Shortcakes will keep for 3 to 4 days at room temperature in a tightly sealed plastic container. The shortcakes come to life when served warm; just pop them in a 275-degree-Fahrenheit oven for 3 to 4 minutes. Before serving, use a serrated knife to cut the shortcakes in half horizontally.

Strawberries are delicious with this recipe. But if you really want to indulge, use raspberries instead and serve with lots of whipped cream. The shortcakes are also great with ice cream.

CHOCOLATE ANGEL FOOD BITES

Yields 4 dozen 1½-inch bites

INGREDIENTS

¾ cup cake flour

¼ cup unsweetened cocoa powder

10 large egg whites

1 teaspoon cream of tartar

¼ teaspoon salt

1 cup granulated sugar

8 ounces plus 4 tablespoons semisweet chocolate mini-morsels

EQUIPMENT

Measuring cups, measuring spoons, sifter, wax paper, 7-quart bowl, hand-held electric mixer, rubber spatula, 4 nonstick 12-cup miniature muffin tins, popsicle stick, plastic cookie storage container with lid

THE CHEF'S TOUCH

Do not grease the muffin tins, because the cakes will not rise properly. Undoubtedly, some batter will stick to the insides of the cups during baking, even with nonstick muffin tins, but they will clean easily with a wipe of a sponge after soaking in warm water for 15 to 20 minutes.

Chocolate Angel Food Bites will keep for 2 to 3 days at room temperature in a tightly sealed plastic container.

These light bites of chocolate heaven are perfect for an afternoon sweet or a late night chocolate snack because they won't weigh you down.

MAKE THE CHOCOLATE ANGEL FOOD BITES

Preheat the oven to 350 degrees Fahrenheit.

In a sifter combine the flour and cocoa powder. Sift onto a large piece of wax paper and set aside until needed.

In a 7-quart bowl, whisk the egg whites, cream of tartar, and salt using a hand-held electric mixer (if you are feeling energetic, use a balloon whisk; mixing time will increase). Whisk on medium until foamy, about 1 minute. Increase the speed to high and whisk for 2 more minutes until the egg whites begin to stiffen. Continue to whisk on high, while gradually adding the sugar, until the egg whites are stiff but not dry, about 4 minutes. Use a rubber spatula to fold in the sifted dry ingredients, followed by 8 ounces chocolate mini-morsels, combining thoroughly.

Portion one heaping tablespoon (a bit more than ½ ounce) of batter into each of the 48 miniature muffin cups. Sprinkle ¼ teaspoon chocolate mini-morsels over the top of each portion of batter. Place the muffin tins on the center rack of the preheated oven and bake for 20 minutes until the tops are dry to the touch. Remove the bites from the oven and cool at room temperature for 30 minutes before removing from the muffin tins. Use a popsicle stick to pop the bites out of the cups (slide the popsicle stick down the inside edge of the cup and once you hit bottom with the stick, lift the stick up and inward at the same time and the muffin should pop right out). Store the bites in a tightly sealed plastic container until ready to serve.

CHOCOLATE NOUGAT SQUARES

Yields 32 1-inch squares

MAKE THE CHOCOLATE NOUGAT SQUARES

Preheat the oven to 325 degrees Fahrenheit.

Toast the peanuts on a baking sheet in the preheated oven until golden brown, about 10 to 12 minutes. Cool to room temperature before using.

Line a loaf pan with plastic wrap. Set aside.

Heat the brown sugar, butter, corn syrup, and cream in a 3-quart saucepan over medium-high heat. Bring to a boil, stirring occasionally to dissolve the sugar. Lower the heat and allow the mixture to simmer, stirring occasionally, for 10 minutes. Remove from the heat and add the unsweetened chocolate, stirring to dissolve. Add the peanuts and stir to combine (the temptation to taste will be great, but don't do it—hot sugar syrup will burn you). Pour the mixture into the prepared loaf pan, using a rubber spatula to spread it evenly. Refrigerate the nougat, uncovered, for 3 hours.

Remove the nougat from the refrigerator and invert it onto a clean, dry cutting board. Remove and discard the plastic wrap. Use a sharp serrated knife to cut the nougat lengthwise into 4 1-inch wide strips, then cut each strip into 8 1-inch squares. For a clean cut, heat the blade of the knife under hot running water and wipe the blade dry before making each slice. I also recommend wearing plastic food handlers' gloves so you don't leave incriminating fingerprints on the candy. Individually wrap each piece of nougat in plastic wrap and refrigerate until ready to serve.

INGREDIENTS

2 cups unsalted peanuts

1 cup tightly packed light brown sugar

¼ pound unsalted butter, cut into 1-ounce pieces

¾ cup dark corn syrup

½ cup heavy cream

2 ounces unsweetened chocolate, chopped into ¼-inch pieces

EQUIPMENT

Measuring cups, cook's knife, cutting board, baking sheet, 9×5×3-inch loaf pan, plastic wrap, 3-quart saucepan, rubber spatula, sharp serrated knife, plastic cookie storage container with lid

THE CHEF'S TOUCH

This candy is easy to make, but it's a tough workout for the jaw. Hopefully this simple recipe will not disappoint those who prefer to labor long and hard for their traditional nougats. Anyway, I think nougat lovers would rather use their jaw muscles to enjoy these delicious Chocolate Nougat Squares now than debate whether it is a classic nougat or not.

Chocolate Nougat Squares will keep for more than a week in the refrigerator when individually wrapped. For a festive touch, wrap each Nougat Square in colored cellophane and tie it with a ribbon. A large serving dish filled with cellophane-wrapped nougats is a dandy sight.

WHITE AND DARK CHOCOLATE DOGWOOD BARK

Yields about 2 pounds

THE CHEF'S TOUCH

My adrenaline surges just at the sight of a 2-pound slab of White and Dark Chocolate Dogwood Bark. I love chocolate in many forms, but Bark is particularly irresistible because of its unmitigated delivery of chocolate flavor.

Since little comes between the consumer and pure chocolate in this recipe, I encourage purchasing the highest-quality chocolate available. Taste-test if you are unfamiliar with a particular manufacturer's brand (this in itself is pure joy). Remember, the Bark will only be as good as the flavor of the chocolate you use.

See "Notes from Ganache Hill" (page 6) for purchasing information on white chocolate.

White and Dark Chocolate Dogwood Bark will keep for several days stored in a tightly sealed plastic container in the refrigerator. Enjoy this candy as it is (accompanied by lots of paper napkins), as a garnish for a bowl of ice cream, or broken and folded into a batch of ice cream. Unfortunately, because the Bark is made with untempered chocolate, it will not travel well.

INGREDIENTS

3 cups pecan halves

6 ounces white chocolate, chopped into ¼-inch pieces

12 ounces semisweet chocolate, chopped into ¼-inch pieces

EQUIPMENT

Measuring cups, cook's knife, cutting board, nonstick baking sheet with sides, double boiler, rubber spatula, 1-quart bowl, 4-quart bowl, plastic cookie storage container with lid

MAKE THE DOGWOOD BARK

Preheat the oven to 325 degrees Fahrenheit.

Toast the pecans on a baking sheet in the preheated oven for 8 minutes. Remove the nuts from the oven and set aside to cool at room temperature until needed.

Heat 1 inch of water in the bottom half of a double boiler over medium heat. With the heat on, place the white chocolate in the top half of the double boiler. Use a rubber spatula to stir the chocolate until completely melted and smooth, about 4 minutes. Transfer the melted chocolate to a 1-quart bowl and set aside.

Thoroughly wash and dry the top half of the double boiler.

Heat 1 inch of water in the bottom half of the double boiler over medium heat. With the heat on, place the semisweet chocolate in the top half of the double boiler. Use a rubber spatula to stir the chocolate until completely melted and smooth, about 6 minutes. Transfer the melted chocolate to a 4-quart bowl. Allow the chocolate to stand at room temperature for 5 minutes before proceeding. Add the pecans to the bowl of melted semisweet chocolate. Use a rubber spatula to fold in the pecans until combined. Pour the chocolate pecan mixture onto a nonstick baking sheet with sides and use a rubber spatula to spread the mixture evenly. Drizzle the white chocolate, one tablespoon at a time, over the entire surface of the chocolate pecan mixture.

Use a rubber spatula to spread and blend the white chocolate into the surface of the chocolate pecan mixture, creating a marbleized effect (be careful not to overblend, which would diminish the marbleized effect). Cool the mixture at room temperature for 30 minutes. Cover the baking sheet with plastic wrap and refrigerate until the bark is hard, about 1 hour. Remove the baking sheet from the refrigerator and transfer the bark to a cutting board. Use a cook's knife to cut the bark into irregular pieces. Refrigerate in a tightly sealed plastic container until ready to use.

CHOCOLATE DOUBLE PEANUT BRITTLE

Yields about 1¼ pounds

INGREDIENTS

¾ cup unsalted peanuts

½ cup semisweet chocolate chips

¼ cup peanut butter flavored chips

2 teaspoons pure vanilla extract

1 teaspoon baking soda

1 cup granulated sugar

½ cup light corn syrup

½ cup water

EQUIPMENT

Measuring cups, measuring spoons, baking sheet, 9×13×2-inch nonstick rectangular baking pan, 1-quart bowl, whisk, 3-quart saucepan, cutting board, sharp cook's knife, plastic cookie storage container with lid

THE CHEF'S TOUCH

Old-fashioned candy seems to be making a comeback. Truth is, peanut brittle has never lost its popularity in some areas of the country. When I am on a road trip, I find the best brittle in the mom-and-pop stores that dot the back roads running parallel to the main highway. I'm afraid that with the introduction of chocolate in this recipe, however, I may start bringing my own supply.

Chocolate Double Peanut Brittle will keep for several days at room temperature in a tightly sealed plastic container. If you eliminate the chocolate and peanut butter chips, it will keep much longer, but why would you want to do that?

MAKE THE CHOCOLATE DOUBLE PEANUT BRITTLE

Preheat the oven to 325 degrees Fahrenheit.

Toast the peanuts on a baking sheet in the preheated oven until golden brown, about 10 to 12 minutes. Remove from the oven and cool to room temperature.

Evenly sprinkle the peanuts, chocolate chips, and finally the peanut butter flavored chips over the bottom of the 9×13×2-inch nonstick baking pan. Set aside.

In a 1-quart bowl, whisk together the vanilla extract and baking soda. Set aside.

Heat the sugar, corn syrup, and water in a 3-quart saucepan over medium-high heat. When hot, stir to dissolve the sugar. Bring to a boil. Continue to boil, whisking frequently, for 15 minutes until very lightly golden in color (if you have a candy thermometer, the temperature should reach 300 degrees Fahrenheit). This is burning hot, so work carefully. Remove from the heat and immediately add the vanilla extract mixture, stirring gently to combine. Pour the hot, syrupy mixture over the peanuts and chips. Tilt the baking pan back and forth, encouraging the hot mixture to flow over the entire surface of the peanuts and chips. Harden the brittle at room temperature for 1 hour, then refrigerate for 1/2 hour. Invert the brittle onto a cutting board and use a cook's knife to cut the brittle into irregular pieces (or use your hands to break it apart). Store the brittle in a tightly sealed plastic container at room temperature until ready to serve.

CHOCOLATE JUNGLE CRUNCH
Yields about 2½ pounds

MAKE THE CHOCOLATE JUNGLE CRUNCH

The process of toasting the peanuts, sunflower kernels, and coconut flakes may appear to be tedious and make the recipe seem longer than it is, but the toasting step is actually quick and easy (you can put all 3 items in the oven at the same time on separate baking sheets) and an important step to the recipe's crunch. Just keep your eye on the clock and pull the items from the oven at the appropriate time.

Preheat the oven to 325 degrees Fahrenheit.

Toast the dried coconut flakes in the preheated oven until lightly golden brown, about 6 to 8 minutes.

Toast the sunflower kernels on a baking sheet in the preheated oven for 10 minutes. Cool to room temperature.

Toast the peanuts on a baking sheet in the preheated oven until golden brown, about 10 to 12 minutes. Cool to room temperature.

Heat 1 inch of water in the bottom half of a double boiler over medium heat. With the heat on, place the semisweet and unsweetened chocolate in the top half of the double boiler. Use a rubber spatula to stir the chocolate until completely melted and smooth, about 6 minutes. Transfer the melted chocolate to a 7-quart bowl. Add the peanuts, ½ cup sunflower kernels, raisins, banana chips, and ½ the amount of coconut. Use a rubber spatula to stir until all the ingredients are combined. Transfer the mixture to a nonstick baking sheet with sides and use a rubber spatula to spread in an even layer. Sprinkle the remaining sunflower kernels and then the remaining coconut over the entire surface of the chocolate mixture. Cool at room temperature for 30 minutes, then refrigerate for 1 hour.

Remove the candy from the refrigerator and invert onto a clean, dry cutting board (it should pop right out of the baking sheet). Use a sharp serrated knife to cut the candy (use a sawing motion) into desired size pieces. Store the candy in a tightly sealed plastic container in the refrigerator. Serve the Chocolate Jungle Crunch in paper candy cups.

INGREDIENTS

4 ounces dried coconut flakes
1 cup unsalted sunflower kernels
1 cup unsalted peanuts
1 pound semisweet chocolate, chopped into ¼-inch pieces
4 ounces unsweetened chocolate, chopped into ¼-inch pieces
1 cup raisins
4 ounces dried banana chips

EQUIPMENT

Measuring cups, cook's knife, cutting board, 3 baking sheets (1 nonstick with sides), double boiler, rubber spatula, 7-quart bowl, sharp serrated knife, plastic cookie storage container with lid

THE CHEF'S TOUCH

You can't sneak around with this goodie. If the noise of the crunch doesn't cause a stampede in your direction, the fragrance of the chocolate and coconut will.

You can find dried coconut flakes at your local specialty grocer or upscale supermarket. Check out the same section where they display dried nuts, fruits, beans, and the like.

Chocolate Jungle Crunch will keep for a week or more stored in a tightly sealed plastic container in the refrigerator.

Note: Photograph appears on page 13.

CHOCOLATE MAPLE WALNUT PRALINE
Yields about 1½ pounds

INGREDIENTS

1½ cups walnut pieces
½   cup pure maple syrup
2   cups granulated sugar
½   teaspoon fresh lemon juice
2   ounces unsweetened chocolate,
    chopped into ¼-inch pieces

EQUIPMENT

Measuring cups, measuring spoons, cook's knife, cutting board, nonstick baking sheet with sides, 1½-quart saucepan, metal spoon, 3-quart saucepan, whisk, sharp serrated knife, plastic cookie storage container with lid

THE CHEF'S TOUCH

Purchase pure maple syrup for this recipe and not the sapless imitation stuff they give you at the pancake house.

Chocolate Maple Walnut Praline will keep for several days at room temperature if stored in a tightly sealed plastic container. Since this type of candy is very susceptible to humidity and moisture, cool and dry conditions are the optimum. The pralines can be refrigerated or frozen, but they will be tacky to the touch. In that case, you can also use the pralines in other confections. Try folding ¼-inch pieces of praline into white chocolate or vanilla ice cream; this will do marvels for the ice cream's texture.

MAKE THE CHOCOLATE MAPLE WALNUT PRALINE

Preheat the oven to 325 degrees Fahrenheit.

Toast the walnuts on a baking sheet in the preheated oven for 8 minutes. Remove from the oven and cool to room temperature.

Heat the maple syrup in a 1½-quart saucepan over medium-high heat. When the syrup begins to boil, reduce the heat to medium and continue to boil as it thickens for 10 minutes, stirring occasionally with a metal spoon. Remove the very hot syrup from the heat. Immediately add the walnuts to the syrup and stir to combine. Transfer the glazed walnuts to a baking sheet with sides. Use the metal spoon to spread the walnuts evenly over one half of the baking sheet. Set aside.

Place the sugar and lemon juice in a 3-quart saucepan. Stir with a whisk to combine (the sugar will resemble moist sand). Caramelize the sugar by heating for 10 to 10 1/2 minutes over medium-high heat, stirring constantly with a wire whisk to break up any lumps (the sugar will first turn clear as it liquefies, then light brown as it caramelizes). Remove the saucepan from the heat, add the unsweetened chocolate, and stir to dissolve. Immediately and carefully pour the chocolate caramelized mixture over the walnuts, covering all the nuts.

Harden at room temperature for at least 30 minutes.

Invert the praline onto a clean, dry cutting board (it should pop right out of the baking sheet). Use a sharp serrated knife to cut the praline (use a sawing motion) into desired size pieces. Store the praline in a tightly sealed plastic container until ready to devour.

ESPRESSO TO GO

Yields about 2½ dozen espresso cups

INGREDIENTS

- ¾ cup heavy cream
- 3 tablespoons instant espresso powder
- ¼ cup granulated sugar
- 4 tablespoons unsalted butter
- 12 ounces semisweet chocolate, chopped into ¼-inch pieces
- 4 ounces unsweetened chocolate, chopped into ¼-inch pieces
- 30 individual chocolate-covered espresso beans

EQUIPMENT

Measuring cups, measuring spoons, cook's knife, cutting board, 1½-quart saucepan, 4-quart bowl, 30 1-ounce foil candy cups, baking sheet, plastic cookie storage container with lid

THE CHEF'S TOUCH

For ease of handling, consider using a 12-cup mini-muffin tin to hold the foil cups when filling them with the liquid ganache. When filling the cups by the tablespoon, use an index finger if necessary to push the ganache out of the tablespoon and into the cups.

The Espresso To Go will keep for several days stored in the refrigerator in a tightly sealed plastic container.

MAKE THE ESPRESSO TO GO

Heat the heavy cream, instant espresso powder, sugar, and butter in a 1½-quart saucepan over medium-high heat. When hot, stir to dissolve the sugar. Bring to a boil. Place the semisweet and unsweetened chocolate in a 4-quart bowl. Pour the boiling cream mixture over the chocolate and allow to stand for 5 minutes. Stir until smooth and, *presto*, espresso ganache.

Place the foil cups on a baking sheet.

Spoon 2 level tablespoons of ganache into each foil cup. Top each cup with a chocolate-covered espresso bean. Refrigerate until firm, about 1 hour. Serve immediately or store in a tightly sealed plastic container in the refrigerator.

ROAD TRIP COOKIES

Yields 1½ dozen 4-inch cookies

- **2½** cups all-purpose flour
- **1** teaspoon baking soda
- **½** teaspoon salt
- **6** ounces semisweet chocolate, chopped into ¼-inch pieces
- **¾** cup granulated sugar
- **¾** cup tightly packed light brown sugar
- **¼** pound unsalted butter at room temperature
- **2** large eggs
- **2** teaspoons pure vanilla extract
- **1½** cups peanut M&M's

EQUIPMENT

Measuring cups, measuring spoons, cook's knife, cutting board, sifter, wax paper, double boiler, rubber spatula, 1-quart bowl, 7-quart bowl, 3 nonstick baking sheets, plastic cookie storage container with lid

THE CHEF'S TOUCH

I have loved peanut M&M's since my childhood, when my mother would ply me with those incomparable candy-coated nuts to keep me happy during frequent road trips. This Road Trip Cookie was born from my love for peanut M&M's and my preference for the earth-hugging road trip.

Road Trip Cookies will keep for several days at room (or car) temperature if stored in a tightly sealed plastic container. For long-term storage, up to several weeks, the cookies may be frozen. Freeze the cookies in a tightly sealed plastic container to avoid dehydration and to protect them from freezer odors.

GET YOUR MOTOR RUNNING

Preheat the oven to 350 degrees Fahrenheit.

In a sifter combine the flour, baking soda, and salt. Sift onto a large piece of wax paper and set aside until needed.

Heat 1 inch of water in the bottom half of a double boiler over medium heat. With the heat on, place the semisweet chocolate in the top half of the double boiler. Use a rubber spatula to stir the chocolate until completely melted and smooth, about 4 to 5 minutes. Transfer to a 1-quart bowl and set aside.

Place the granulated sugar, light brown sugar, and butter in a 7-quart bowl. Use a stiff rubber spatula (or a wooden spoon) to cream the ingredients together until smooth. Add the eggs and vanilla extract and mix to incorporate. Add the melted chocolate and mix until combined. Add the sifted dry ingredients and thoroughly combine. Add the M&M's, mixing to incorporate.

Using 3 heaping tablespoons of dough for each cookie (approximately 3 ounces), portion 6 cookies, evenly spaced, onto each of 3 nonstick baking sheets (this is a hefty cookie, so don't crowd). Place the baking sheets on the top and center racks of the preheated oven and bake for 14 minutes. Remove the cookies from the oven and cool to room temperature on the baking sheets, about 30 minutes. Store the cooled cookies in a tightly sealed plastic cookie container until ready to serve.

COCOA VAN GO-GOS
Yields about 4 dozen free-form cookies

MAKE THE COCOA VAN GO-GOS

Preheat the oven to 325 degrees Fahrenheit.

In a sifter combine the flour and cocoa powder. Sift onto a large piece of wax paper and set aside until needed.

Line 4 baking sheets with parchment paper.

Place the butter, light brown sugar, and salt in a 7-quart bowl. Use a stiff rubber spatula (or wooden spoon) to mix the ingredients together until smooth. Add the egg whites and vanilla extract and combine until incorporated. Add the sifted dry ingredients and blend together until the mixture is very smooth and thoroughly combined.

Using a heaping teaspoon (approximately ⅓-ounce) of batter for each cookie, portion 12 cookies, evenly spaced, onto each of 4 parchment-lined baking sheets. Use an index finger (a popsicle stick or offset cake spatula will also do) to spread each portion of batter into a free-form design measuring about 3 square inches for each cookie (be creative and have fun with this). Place the baking sheets on the top and center racks of the preheated oven and bake for 14 minutes. Remove the cookies from the oven and allow to cool at room temperature for 30 minutes before handling. Store the cookies in a tightly sealed plastic container until ready to serve.

INGREDIENTS

1	cup all-purpose flour
2	tablespoons unsweetened cocoa powder
¼	pound unsalted butter at room temperature
½	cup tightly packed light brown sugar
¼	teaspoon salt
2	large egg whites
1	teaspoon pure vanilla extract

EQUIPMENT

Measuring cups, measuring spoons, sifter, wax paper, 4 baking sheets, parchment paper, 7-quart bowl, rubber spatula, plastic cookie storage container with lid

THE CHEF'S TOUCH

Let the artist in you come out with these cookies. Making these gems is better than finger painting because you can lick your fingers when you're done.

For a finishing touch, sprinkle cocoa powder and confectioners' sugar onto the cookies.

The Cocoa Van Go-Gos will stay crisp for 2 to 3 days in a tightly sealed plastic container at room temperature.

Serve the Cocoa Van Go-Gos with ice cream; they also make a very light accompaniment to a late afternoon espresso.

Use an index finger to spread each portion of batter into a free-form design.

Family Secrets

OPPOSITE: **Mrs. D's Chocolate Chip Cookies (see page 43)** ABOVE: **Danielle's Cocoa Ginger Snaps (see page 42)**

CONNIE'S COCOA COFFEE TOFFEE COOKIES

Yields 4 dozen 3-inch cookies

ALMOND TOFFEE

2	cups whole almonds
1	cup granulated sugar
½	pound unsalted butter, cut into 1-ounce pieces
¼	cup water
¼	teaspoon salt

COCOA COFFEE COOKIE BATTER

4	tablespoons instant espresso powder
1	tablespoon pure vanilla extract
1	teaspoon almond extract
3½	cups all-purpose flour
½	cup unsweetened cocoa powder
2	teaspoons baking soda
1	teaspoon salt
¾	pound unsalted butter, cut into 1-ounce pieces
1	cup tightly packed light brown sugar
½	cup granulated sugar
4	large eggs

EQUIPMENT

Measuring cups, measuring spoons, cook's knife, cutting board, 4 nonstick baking sheets (1 with sides), 3-quart saucepan, whisk, candy thermometer, wooden spoon, 1-quart bowl, sifter, wax paper, table-model electric mixer with paddle, rubber spatula, plastic cookie storage container with lid

MAKE THE TOFFEE

Preheat the oven to 350 degrees Fahrenheit.

Toast the whole almonds on a baking sheet in the preheated oven for 12 minutes. Remove the nuts from the oven and set aside to cool at room temperature until needed.

Heat 1 cup granulated sugar, ½ pound butter, ¼ cup water, and ¼ teaspoon salt in a 3-quart saucepan over medium-high heat, stirring constantly with a whisk until the mixture comes to a boil, about 3½ to 4 minutes. Continue to boil the mixture, stirring constantly, until it reaches a temperature of 300 degrees Fahrenheit and appears light blond in color, about 9 minutes (work carefully—at 300 degrees, this is really hot stuff). Immediately add the whole toasted almonds and use a wooden spoon to fold them in until thoroughly combined; you need to work quickly here because the toffee will shortly begin to harden and become difficult to pour. Pour the toffee onto the baking sheet with sides, and use a wooden spoon to smooth it out over the surface of the sheet (no need to cover the whole surface, but avoid having the almonds on top of each other). Cool the toffee at room temperature for 20 minutes, until it has hardened.

Once hardened, transfer the toffee to a cutting board, and use a cook's knife to chop it into ¼-inch pieces. This will yield 5 cups of chopped toffee (which is more than enough, so feel free to sample a piece or two).

MAKE THE COOKIES

Preheat the oven to 350 degrees Fahrenheit.

Combine the espresso powder, vanilla extract, and almond extract in a 1-quart bowl. Stir to dissolve the espresso powder. Set aside until needed.

In a sifter combine the flour, cocoa powder, baking soda, and salt. Sift onto a large piece of wax paper and set aside until needed.

Place ¾ pound butter, the brown sugar, and ½ cup granulated sugar in the bowl of an electric mixer fitted with a paddle. Beat on medium for 2 minutes until soft. Use a rubber spatula to scrape down the sides of the bowl, then beat on medium for 2 more minutes until fairly smooth. Scrape down the bowl once more. Add the eggs, one at a time, beating on medium for 1 minute and scraping down the bowl after each addition. Add the espresso powder mixture and mix on high for 1 minute. Operate the mixer on low while slowly adding the sifted dry ingredients until thoroughly combined, about 30 seconds. Add the chopped toffee and mix on low for another 30 seconds until incorporated. Remove the bowl from the mixer and use a rubber spatula to finish mixing the ingredients until thoroughly combined.

Using a heaping tablespoon for each cookie (approximately 1½ ounces), portion 12 cookies, evenly spaced, onto each of 4 nonstick baking sheets. Place the baking sheets on the top and center racks of the preheated oven and bake for 12 minutes, rotating the sheets from top to center halfway through the baking time (at that time also turn each sheet 180 degrees). Remove the cookies from the oven and allow to cool to room temperature on the baking sheets, about 30 minutes. Store the cooled cookies in a tightly sealed plastic container until ready to serve.

THE CHEF'S TOUCH

I'm still doing penance for the recipe called "Connie's Sticky Buns," from Desserts To Die For, *after explaining on broadcast television that the inspiration for its title came from my wife Connie's college nickname. So I now redeem myself by naming this delicious, sometimes unpredictable, but always intriguing cookie after her.*

A candy thermometer is an important piece of equipment for making toffee. Failure to reach the "hard crack" stage at 300 degrees Fahrenheit will yield a sticky, pliable mass of toffee rather than an appealingly brittle, crunchy sheet of candy.

Connie's Cocoa Coffee Toffee Cookies will keep for several days at room temperature if stored in a tightly sealed plastic container. For long-term storage, up to several weeks, the cookies may be frozen in a tightly sealed plastic container to prevent dehydration and to protect them from freezer odors.

DANIELLE'S COCOA GINGER SNAPS

Yields about 2 dozen 6-inch long snaps

THE CHEF'S TOUCH

How sweet it is that my daughter Danielle graduated from my alma mater, The Culinary Institute of America. When I graduated in 1965, all I wanted to do was cook. At that time, the thought of having a daughter follow in my footsteps was more remote than calculus. Today, however, I revel in the knowledge that my career inspired Danielle to enter the food-service world, which she did after acquiring a studio-art degree from the College of William & Mary. Now that she has graduated and moved on, I shall miss seeing her regularly. Luckily, I have the delicate cookies she perfected in 1986 when we cooked together on a barge in Burgundy (she was just sixteen years old) to remind me of her. I guess I should have known then that Danielle might end up "in the business."

Danielle's Cocoa Ginger Snaps will keep for several days at room temperature if stored in a tightly sealed plastic container. The crisp texture of the cookie is affected by humidity, so be sure to store them in a sealed container as soon as they have cooled to help them keep their crunch.

Note: Photograph appears on page 39.

INGREDIENTS

⅔ cup all-purpose flour
2 tablespoons unsweetened cocoa powder
1 teaspoon ground ginger
½ teaspoon salt
½ pound unsalted butter, cut into 1-ounce pieces
1½ cups granulated sugar
1 tablespoon brandy

EQUIPMENT

Measuring cups, measuring spoons, cook's knife, cutting board, 2 baking sheets, parchment paper, sifter, wax paper, table-model electric mixer with paddle, rubber spatula, 4 chopsticks, paper towels, plastic cookie storage container with lid

PREPARE THE COCOA GINGER SNAPS

Preheat the oven to 350 degrees Fahrenheit.

Line 2 baking sheets with parchment paper. Set aside.

In a sifter combine the flour, cocoa powder, ground ginger, and salt. Sift onto a large piece of wax paper and set aside until needed.

Place the butter, sugar, and brandy in the bowl of an electric mixer fitted with a paddle. Beat on medium for 3 minutes until smooth. Use a rubber spatula to scrape down the sides of the bowl, then beat on high for 1 additional minute until very smooth. Scrape down the sides of the bowl. Add the sifted dry ingredients and mix on low for 15 seconds, then increase the mixer speed to medium and beat for 30 seconds until incorporated. Remove the bowl from the mixer and use a rubber spatula to finish mixing the batter until it is thoroughly combined.

Using 1 slightly heaping tablespoon (just short of 1 ounce) of batter for each snap, portion 2 snaps, evenly spaced (allow plenty of space between each portion of batter since it spreads on its own during baking), on each of the 2 baking sheets. Place the baking sheets on the center rack of the preheated oven and bake for 8 to 9 minutes until the batter stops bubbling and the edges darken. Remove a baking sheet from the oven (leave the other baking sheet in the oven with the oven door open). Immediately remove the parchment paper with the snaps from the baking sheet. Invert the snaps (parchment paper side up) onto a clean, flat surface, then peel the parchment paper away from the snaps. Moving quickly—you've got work to do, so don't get distracted by the richness of the aroma—roll each snap into a cigar-shaped cylinder around a chopstick, then place on a paper towel. Repeat this procedure with the remaining 2 snaps.

Allow the snaps to cool on the paper towels for 5 minutes before removing the chopsticks.

Portion the remaining snaps onto new sheets of parchment paper, and use the same procedure and baking time until all the batter has been used. Allow all the snaps to cool to room temperature before storing in a tightly sealed plastic container until ready to serve.

MRS. D'S CHOCOLATE CHIP COOKIES
Yields 2 dozen 4-inch cookies

INGREDIENTS

4 cups all-purpose flour

1½ teaspoons baking soda

½ teaspoon salt

½ pound unsalted butter, cut into 1-ounce pieces

2 cups tightly packed dark brown sugar

2 large eggs

2 tablespoons dark rum

1 teaspoon pure vanilla extract

24 ounces semisweet chocolate chips

EQUIPMENT

Measuring cups, measuring spoons, cook's knife, cutting board, sifter, wax paper, table-model electric mixer with paddle, rubber spatula, 4 nonstick baking sheets, plastic cookie storage container with lid

THE CHEF'S TOUCH

The question I inevitably hear is, "What's your favorite recipe in the book?" With one of my mother's recipes in this book, that question is easily and honestly answered: of course, Mrs. D's Chocolate Chip Cookies. This is my favorite recipe and not because I would sound ungrateful otherwise. As a toddler, I teethed on this cookie (along with her fudge). As time passed, it greeted me after school and brought my family together around the kitchen table. When I was in the armed services, this cookie brought me joy in Vietnam and put a smile on the faces of my U.S. Marine buddies desperate for a taste of home. With a cookie like this from Mom, I don't know why anyone needs apple pie.

Mrs. D and her family love crisp cookies. If your preference is for a soft-baked cookie, then bake them for only 20 minutes at 325 degrees Fahrenheit.

Mrs. D's Chocolate Chip Cookies will keep forever, or close to it, when held at room temperature in a tightly sealed plastic container (but if you are going to keep them for that long you shouldn't be reading this book). For long-term storage, up to several weeks, the cookies may be frozen in a tightly sealed plastic container to prevent dehydration and to protect them from freezer odors.

Note: Photograph appears on page 38.

MAKE MRS. D'S CHOCOLATE CHIP COOKIES

Preheat the oven to 300 degrees Fahrenheit.

In a sifter combine the flour, baking soda, and salt. Sift onto a large piece of wax paper and set aside until needed.

Place the butter and brown sugar in the bowl of an electric mixer fitted with a paddle. Beat on medium for 4 minutes until soft. Use a rubber spatula to scrape down the sides of the bowl, then add the eggs, dark rum, and vanilla extract and beat on medium for 1 minute until combined. Scrape down the bowl once again. Operate the mixer on low while gradually adding the sifted dry ingredients until incorporated, about 1 minute. Add the chocolate chips and mix on low for 30 seconds. Remove the bowl from the mixer and use a rubber spatula to finish mixing the dough until thoroughly combined.

Using 2 heaping tablespoons of dough (just shy of 3 ounces) for each cookie, portion 6 cookies, evenly spaced, onto each of 4 nonstick baking sheets. Place the baking sheets on the top and center racks of the preheated oven and bake for 28 to 30 minutes until dry to the touch, rotating the sheets from top to center halfway through the baking time (at that time also turn each sheet 180 degrees). Remove the cookies from the oven and allow to cool on the baking sheets for 30 minutes. Store the cookies in a tightly sealed plastic container until ready to serve.

JIM SEU'S CHOCOLATE GANACHIOLIS

Yields 4 dozen 2½-inch cookies

INGREDIENTS

GANACHIOLI DOUGH

3 cups all-purpose flour

¾ cup semolina flour

1 teaspoon baking soda

½ teaspoon salt

½ pound unsalted butter, cut into 1-ounce pieces

1 cup granulated sugar

3 large eggs

½ teaspoon pure vanilla extract

4 tablespoons extra virgin olive oil

4 tablespoons turbinado sugar (Sugar in the Raw)

GANACHE FILLING

1 cup pine nuts

⅓ cup heavy cream

½ tablespoon granulated sugar

6 ounces semisweet chocolate, chopped into ¼-inch pieces

EQUIPMENT

Measuring cups, measuring spoons, cook's knife, cutting board, sifter, wax paper, table-model electric mixer with paddle, rubber spatula, plastic wrap, 4 nonstick baking sheets, 1½-quart saucepan, 1-quart bowl, rolling pin, pastry brush, plastic cookie storage container with lid

MAKE THE GANACHIOLI DOUGH

In a sifter combine 2½ cups all-purpose flour, semolina flour, baking soda, and salt. Sift onto a large piece of wax paper and set aside.

Place the butter and 1 cup granulated sugar in the bowl of an electric mixer fitted with a paddle. Beat on medium for 2 minutes. Use a rubber spatula to scrape down the sides of the bowl, then beat on high for 2 minutes. Scrape down the sides of the bowl once again. Add the eggs, one at a time, beating on medium for 1 minute and scraping down the sides of the bowl after each addition. Add the vanilla extract and beat on high for 1 minute. Operate the mixer on low while gradually adding the sifted dry ingredients; mix for 1 minute. Remove the bowl from the mixer and use a rubber spatula to finish mixing the dough until thoroughly combined. Divide the dough into 2 equal pieces and wrap each tightly in plastic wrap. Refrigerate for 2 hours.

MAKE THE GANACHE FILLING

Preheat the oven to 375 degrees Fahrenheit.

Toast the pine nuts on a baking sheet in the preheated oven until golden brown, about 3 to 4 minutes. Cool the pine nuts to room temperature before using a cook's knife to chop them finely.

Heat the heavy cream and ½ tablespoon granulated sugar in a 1½-quart saucepan over medium-high heat. When hot, stir to dissolve the sugar. Bring to a boil. Place the semisweet chocolate in a 1-quart bowl. Pour the boiling cream over the chocolate and allow to stand for 5 minutes. Stir until smooth. Add the chopped pine nuts and stir to incorporate. Refrigerate the ganache filling until ready to use.

ASSEMBLE AND BAKE THE GANACHIOLIS

Remove 1 piece of the chilled dough from the refrigerator; discard the plastic wrap. Place the dough onto a clean, dry, lightly floured work surface. Roll the dough (using the remaining ½ cup of flour, as necessary, to prevent the dough from sticking) into a rectangle approximately 16 inches long and 12 inches wide. Use a cook's knife to trim the edges of the dough into an even rectangle 16 inches long and 12 inches wide. Cut the rectangle in half widthwise creating 2 8×12-inch pieces. Cut each piece twice lengthwise at 4-inch intervals, and 3 times widthwise at 2-inch intervals. This will yield 24 rectangles 4 inches long and 2 inches wide. Portion one teaspoon of ganache filling, centered, on one half of each rectangle. Carefully fold the opposite half of the rectangle over the filling. Use your fingers to gently press down on the edges, and then use a fork to crimp them and form a seal. Transfer the filled Ganachioli cookies to 2 nonstick baking sheets, 12 evenly spaced Ganachiolis per sheet.

Repeat the preceding process with the remaining half of the dough.

Lightly brush each Ganachioli cookie with olive oil, and then sprinkle each with turbinado sugar. Place the baking sheets on the top and center racks of the preheated oven and bake for 11 to 12 minutes, rotating the sheets from top to center halfway through the baking time (at that time also turn each sheet 180 degrees). Remove the cookies from the oven and allow to cool to room temperature on the baking sheets, about 30 minutes. Store the cookies in a tightly sealed plastic container until ready to serve.

THE CHEF'S TOUCH

Upon graduation from the College of William & Mary, my friend Jim Seu decided to open his own restaurant, The Colonial. Located just a few yards away from historic Colonial Williamsburg, the restaurant has become an institution. Jim's soul, however, is in Italy. He suggested this ravioli-style cookie, which is similar to something his Sardinian mother made for him as a child. I think the ganache filling with the pine nuts sets this cookie apart from other similarly shaped cookies, which generally have fruit filling.

Pine nuts are quite oily, so I recommend that you chop them by hand with a cook's knife rather than using a food processor. Make sure to cool the nuts to room temperature before chopping. Since they have a high natural oil content, I recommend purchasing only as many pine nuts as needed because they turn rancid in a short period of time. If you do have extra pine nuts on hand, do as we do at the Trellis and store them in the freezer.

Semolina flour, also sold as pasta flour, gives this cookie dough its unique character. Most supermarkets now carry semolina flour in the same section as other flours (also look for it in the international foods section).

Jim Seu's Chocolate Ganachiolis will keep for 3 to 4 days at room temperature if stored in a tightly sealed plastic container. Don't refrigerate or freeze them, however, since both the exterior and interior are altered when held at temperatures other than room temperature.

HESSIE RAE'S CHOCOLATE PECAN TART COOKIES

Yields 3 dozen 1½-inch cookies

INGREDIENTS

TART COOKIE DOUGH

½ pound unsalted butter at room temperature

½ pound cream cheese, cut into 1-ounce pieces, softened

2½ cups all-purpose flour

CHOCOLATE PECAN FILLING

1½ cups pecans

4 ounces semisweet chocolate, chopped into ¼-inch pieces

1 cup tightly packed dark brown sugar

2 large eggs

1 tablespoon pure vanilla extract

¼ teaspoon salt

EQUIPMENT

Cook's knife, cutting board, measuring cups, measuring spoons, table-model electric mixer with paddle and balloon whip, rubber spatula, wax paper, 3 nonstick 12-cup miniature muffin tins, 3 nonstick baking sheets, food processor with metal blade, double boiler, 1-quart bowl, plastic cookie storage container with lid

MAKE THE TART COOKIE DOUGH

Preheat the oven to 350 degrees Fahrenheit.

Place the butter and cream cheese in the bowl of an electric mixer fitted with a paddle. Beat on medium for 1 minute. Use a rubber spatula to scrape down the sides of the bowl, then beat on medium for 1 more minute until smooth. Scrape down the bowl once again. Operate the mixer on low while gradually adding the flour until a loose dough is formed (the dough will be slightly crumbly), about 45 seconds. Remove the dough from the mixer and form it into a smooth round ball, then divide it into 36 tablespoon-size pieces (approximately ¾ ounce per piece) onto a large piece of wax paper. Place a portion into each miniature muffin tin cup. Use your thumb to individually press each dough portion first into the bottom and then onto the sides of each cup (the dough should extend above the rim of the cup by about ¼ inch). Set aside at room temperature while making the filling.

MAKE THE CHOCOLATE PECAN FILLING

Toast the pecans on a baking sheet in the preheated oven for 10 minutes. Cool the nuts to room temperature.

Process the pecans in the bowl of a food processor fitted with a metal blade for 10 seconds, until finely chopped.

Heat 1 inch of water in the bottom half of a double boiler over medium heat. With the heat on, place the semisweet chocolate in the top half of the double boiler. Use a rubber spatula to stir the chocolate until completely melted and smooth, about 3 minutes. Transfer the melted chocolate to a 1-quart bowl and set aside until needed.

Place the dark brown sugar and the eggs in the bowl of an electric mixer fitted with a balloon whip. Whisk on medium for 1 minute. Use a rubber spatula to scrape down the sides of the bowl. Add the vanilla extract and the salt, and whisk on medium for 1 more minute. Stop the mixer and add the melted chocolate; whisk on low for 30 seconds. Remove the bowl from the mixer and add the chopped pecans. Use a rubber spatula to finish mixing the filling until thoroughly combined. Place a level tablespoon of the filling into each tart shell.

BAKE THE CHOCOLATE PECAN TART COOKIES

Place the muffin tins on baking sheets, then place on the top and center racks of the preheated oven and bake for 34 to 36 minutes until the crust turns lightly brown. Remove the cookies from the oven and allow to cool in the muffin tins for 10 minutes. Remove the cookies from the muffin tins and allow to cool to room temperature before storing in a tightly sealed plastic container until ready to serve.

THE CHEF'S TOUCH

Having five sisters myself, I can appreciate my assistant Jon Pierre's attachment to his older twin sisters, Stephanie Rae and Melanie Mae. Stephanie (or Hessie, as Jon calls her) had a particularly strong culinary influence on him in spite of the inevitable foil-wrapped tuna sandwiches she would pack in his lunch bucket. Next to the mushy tuna would appear crunchy sugar cookies, chewy brownies, or Hessie Rae's Chocolate Pecan Tart Cookies, Jon Pierre's favorite. Even today, Jon Pierre looks forward to the Christmas package of her tart cookies, which arrive in checkbook boxes, eight perfect cookies to the box.

Depending on your pantry supply or budget you may use either pecan pieces or pecan halves for the filling recipe.

Hessie Rae's Chocolate Pecan Tart Cookies will keep for 2 to 3 days at room temperature if stored in a tightly sealed plastic container. Refrigeration or freezing is not recommended, as it dramatically alters the texture of the filling.

AUNTIE POUGE'S COCOA BUTTER FLUFFIES

Yields 4 dozen 1¾-inch cookies

THE CHEF'S TOUCH

Everyone should have an Auntie Pouge. In this case, the eponymous auntie belongs to my assistant Jon Pierre. According to him, Auntie Pouge has always enjoyed the good life. Fortunate enough to have "help," she has never spent much time in the kitchen. However, at holiday time, she is wont to bake up some cookies. This recipe is indulgent in its use of butter, but as Ogden Nash said, "there's nothing the matter with butter ...the warmest of greetings I utter."

Auntie Pouge's Cocoa Butter Fluffies are best enjoyed within a day or two of baking, perhaps served, upon Auntie Pouge's recommendation, with a glass of port. Store them in a tightly sealed plastic container.

INGREDIENTS

¾ pound unsalted butter, cut into
   1-ounce pieces
½ cup granulated sugar
2 tablespoons heavy cream
1 teaspoon pure vanilla extract
2½ cups all-purpose flour
½ teaspoon salt
¼ cup confectioners' sugar
¼ cup unsweetened cocoa powder

EQUIPMENT

Cook's knife, cutting board, measuring cups, measuring spoons, table-model electric mixer with paddle, rubber spatula, wax paper, 4 nonstick baking sheets, sifter, spatula, plastic cookie storage container with lid

AUNTIE SAYS START COOKING

Preheat the oven to 325 degrees Fahrenheit.

Place the butter and sugar in the bowl of an electric mixer fitted with a paddle. Beat on medium for 4 minutes. Use a rubber spatula to scrape down the sides of the bowl, then beat on medium for an additional 4 minutes. Scrape down the bowl again. Add the heavy cream and vanilla extract and beat on medium for 2 minutes. Scrape down the bowl once more. Operate the mixer on low while gradually adding the flour and salt, and mix for 1 minute. Remove the bowl from the mixer and use a rubber spatula to finish mixing the dough until thoroughly combined.

Divide the cookie dough into 48 level tablespoon–size pieces (slightly more than ½ ounce for each piece) onto a large piece of wax paper. Gently roll each portion in the palms of your hands to form a smooth ball. Divide the dough balls onto 4 nonstick baking sheets, 12 evenly spaced balls per sheet. Use your fingers to gently press and slightly flatten each ball of dough. Place the baking sheets on the top and center racks of the preheated oven and bake for 10 to 12 minutes, until very lightly browned, rotating the sheets from top to center halfway through the baking time (at that time also turn each sheet 180 degrees).

While the cookies are baking, combine in a sifter the confectioners' sugar and the cocoa powder. Set aside.

Remove the cookies from the oven and allow to stand for 2 minutes (so the cookies are slightly firm before handling). Use a spatula to transfer the cookies onto a large piece of wax paper. Dust the cookies uniformly with half the amount of combined confectioners' sugar and cocoa (this is quite a sight). Allow the cookies to stand untouched for 30 minutes before uniformly dusting them with the remaining sugar and cocoa powder (this is really a remarkable sight). Store the cookies in a tightly sealed plastic container until ready to serve.

LESTER'S DOUBLE CHUNK BUTTERSCOTCH BROWNIES

Yields 2 dozen 2-inch brownies

INGREDIENTS

1 cup all-purpose flour

1½ teaspoons baking powder

½ teaspoon salt

½ pound unsalted butter, melted

1½ cups tightly packed dark brown sugar

2 large eggs

1 teaspoon pure vanilla extract

4 ounces semisweet chocolate, chopped into ¼-inch chunks

4 ounces white chocolate, chopped into ¼-inch chunks

MAKE THE BROWNIES

Preheat the oven to 350 degrees Fahrenheit.

In a sifter combine the flour, baking powder, and salt. Sift onto a large piece of wax paper and set aside until needed.

Place the butter and brown sugar in a 7-quart bowl and whisk to combine. Add the eggs and vanilla extract and whisk until smooth. Add the sifted dry ingredients and use a rubber spatula to incorporate. Add the semisweet and white chocolate chunks and stir to incorporate. Pour the batter into the nonstick baking pan and bake on the center rack of the preheated oven for 25 minutes until set in the center. Remove the pan from the oven and allow to cool at room temperature for 1 hour before cutting.

Use a serrated knife with a rounded tip to cut the brownie into 24 2-inch squares. For a clean cut, heat the blade of the knife under hot running water and wipe the blade dry before making each cut. Serve immediately or store in a tightly sealed plastic container.

EQUIPMENT

Measuring cups, measuring spoons, 1½-quart saucepan, cook's knife, cutting board, sifter, wax paper, 7-quart bowl, whisk, rubber spatula, 9×13×2-inch nonstick rectangular baking pan, serrated knife with rounded tip, plastic cookie storage container with lid

THE CHEF'S TOUCH

Students of the Culinary Institute of America serve a five-month externship midway through their schooling to give them valuable hands-on experience. The Trellis has enthusiastically employed externs since we opened in 1980, benefiting from their spirit and curiosity. Lucky for us, Jonathan Lester served his externship at the Trellis while this book was in progress. My assistant Jon Pierre convinced Jonathan that he could bring fame (if not fortune) to the Lester clan if he would share the recipe for his family's famous Butterscotch Brownies. Jonathan gives credit to his great aunt Betty Lester as the creator of the original Butterscotch Brownie recipe, and to his mother, Priscilla, for perfecting it with the addition of chocolate.

See "Notes From Ganache Hill" for purchasing information on white chocolate.

Lester's Double Chunk Butterscotch Brownies will keep for several days at room temperature if stored in a tightly sealed plastic container. I love them chilled, and they can be kept refrigerated for a week or so covered with plastic wrap. For long-term storage, up to several weeks, the brownies may be frozen in a tightly sealed plastic container to prevent dehydration and to protect them from freezer odors. Thaw before serving.

LETHA'S BUTTERMILK PECAN BROWNIES WITH BROWN BUTTER ICING

Yields 2 dozen 2-inch brownies

INGREDIENTS

BUTTERMILK PECAN BROWNIE BATTER

2	cups pecans
1¼	cups all-purpose flour
½	teaspoon baking soda
1	teaspoon salt
6	ounces chilled unsalted butter, cut into 1-ounce pieces
4	ounces unsweetened chocolate, chopped into ¼-inch pieces
1	cup granulated sugar
3	large eggs
3	tablespoons dark corn syrup
1	teaspoon pure vanilla extract
½	cup nonfat buttermilk

BROWN BUTTER ICING

¼	pound unsalted butter, cut into 1-ounce pieces
4	ounces semisweet chocolate, chopped into ¼-inch pieces
2	cups confectioners' sugar
4	tablespoons heavy cream

EQUIPMENT

Measuring cups, measuring spoons, cook's knife, cutting board, baking sheet, sifter, wax paper, double boiler, rubber spatula, 2 1-quart bowls, electric mixer with paddle, 9×13×2-inch rectangular nonstick baking pan, nonstick sauté pan, cake spatula, serrated knife with rounded tip, plastic cookie storage container with lid

MAKE THE BUTTERMILK PECAN BROWNIES

Preheat the oven to 325 degrees Fahrenheit.

Toast the pecans on a baking sheet in the preheated oven for 6 to 8 minutes. Cool the nuts to room temperature before chopping into ¼-inch pieces with a cook's knife.

In a sifter combine the flour, baking soda, and salt. Sift onto a large piece of wax paper and set aside until needed.

Heat 1 inch of water in the bottom half of a double boiler over medium heat. With the heat on, place 6 ounces butter and the unsweetened chocolate in the top half of the double boiler. Use a rubber spatula to stir the butter and chocolate until completely melted and smooth, about 6 to 7 minutes. Transfer the melted butter and chocolate mixture to a 1-quart bowl and set aside until needed.

Place the granulated sugar, eggs, dark corn syrup, and vanilla extract in the bowl of an electric mixer fitted with a paddle. Beat on medium for 4 minutes until smooth. Use a rubber spatula to scrape down the sides of the bowl, then continue to beat on medium for 2 more minutes until very smooth. Stop the mixer and add the melted butter and chocolate mixture and beat on medium for 1 minute until combined. Operate the mixer on low while gradually adding the sifted dry ingredients, followed by the buttermilk and then the pecans; mix for 1 minute until combined. Remove the bowl from the mixer and use a rubber spatula to finish mixing the batter until thoroughly combined.

Pour the batter into the 9×13×2-inch nonstick baking pan. Use a rubber spatula to spread the batter in an even layer. Bake on the center rack of the preheated oven until a toothpick inserted in the center comes out clean, about 35 minutes. Remove the pan from the oven and allow to cool at room temperature for 1 hour before preparing the icing.

MAKE THE BROWN BUTTER ICING

Heat a nonstick sauté pan over high heat. When the pan is very hot, add ¼ pound butter and brown evenly, about 3 to 4 minutes (be sure to stay with the pan, shaking it back and forth to promote even browning, or the butter will go from brown to burnt in seconds). Immediately transfer the brown butter to a 1-quart bowl and hold at room temperature for 15 minutes.

Heat 1 inch of water in the bottom half of a double boiler over medium heat. With the heat on, place the semisweet chocolate in the top half of the double boiler. Use a rubber spatula to stir the chocolate until completely melted and smooth, about 3 to 4 minutes. Transfer the melted chocolate to a 1-quart bowl and set aside until needed.

Place the brown butter and the confectioners' sugar in the bowl of an electric mixer fitted with a paddle. Beat on medium for 4 minutes until smooth. Use a rubber spatula to scrape down the sides of the bowl, then add the melted chocolate and the heavy cream and beat on medium until combined, about 1 minute. Remove the bowl from the mixer and use a rubber spatula to finish mixing the icing until thoroughly combined and smooth.

Use a cake spatula to evenly spread the icing over the entire surface of the brownie. Refrigerate the iced brownie for 30 minutes before cutting. Use a serrated knife with a rounded tip to cut the brownie into 24 2-inch squares. For a clean cut, heat the blade of the knife under hot running water and wipe the blade dry before making each cut. Serve immediately, or store in a tightly sealed plastic container.

MOM'S CHOCOLATE BANANA RAISIN YOGURT COOKIES WITH YOGURT ICING

Yields 3 dozen 3-inch cookies

INGREDIENTS

CHOCOLATE BANANA RAISIN YOGURT COOKIE BATTER

2	cups all-purpose flour
¾	teaspoon baking soda
¼	teaspoon salt
4	ounces semisweet chocolate, chopped into ¼-inch pieces
¾	cup granulated sugar
¼	pound unsalted butter, cut into 1-ounce pieces
1	large egg
1	teaspoon pure vanilla extract
½	pound ripe bananas, peeled
½	cup plain low-fat yogurt
1	cup raisins

YOGURT ICING

1½	cups confectioners' sugar
2	tablespoons plain low-fat yogurt
1	teaspoon pure vanilla extract

EQUIPMENT

Measuring cups, measuring spoons, cook's knife, cutting board, sifter, wax paper, double boiler, rubber spatula, 1-quart bowl, table-model electric mixer with paddle, 3 nonstick baking sheets, whisk, plastic cookie storage container with lid

MAKE THE CHOCOLATE BANANA RAISIN YOGURT COOKIES

Preheat the oven to 375 degrees Fahrenheit.

In a sifter combine the flour, baking soda, and salt. Sift onto a large piece of wax paper and set aside until needed.

Heat 1 inch of water in the bottom half of a double boiler over medium heat. With the heat on, place the semisweet chocolate in the top half of the double boiler. Use a rubber spatula to stir the chocolate until completely melted and smooth, about 4 minutes. Transfer the melted chocolate to a 1-quart bowl and set aside until needed (the smidgen of chocolate in this recipe goes a long way).

Place the sugar and butter in the bowl of an electric mixer fitted with a paddle. Beat on medium for 4 minutes. Use a rubber spatula to scrape down the sides of the bowl, then continue to beat on medium for 1 more minute. Add the egg, 1 teaspoon vanilla extract, and the banana and beat on medium for 1 minute. Scrape down the bowl. Add the melted chocolate and ½ cup yogurt and beat on medium for 1 minute. Operate the mixer on low while gradually adding the sifted dry ingredients, followed by the raisins, allowing to mix for 1 minute. Remove the bowl from the mixer and use a rubber spatula to finish mixing the dough until thoroughly combined.

Using a heaping tablespoon of dough (approximately 1¼ ounce) for each cookie, portion 12 cookies, evenly spaced, onto each of 3 nonstick baking sheets. Place the baking sheets on the top and center racks of the preheated oven and bake for 10 minutes, rotating the sheets from top to center halfway through the baking time (at that time also turn each sheet 180 degrees). Remove the cookies from the oven and cool to room temperature on the baking sheets, about 30 minutes.

MAKE THE YOGURT ICING

Whisk together the confectioners' sugar, 2 tablespoons yogurt, and 1 teaspoon vanilla extract in a 1-quart bowl until thoroughly combined.

Drizzle 1 teaspoonful of icing over each cookie. Store the cooled cookies in a tightly sealed plastic container until ready to serve.

Another of our talented Culinary Institute of America externs, Jeremy Noye, offered to submit one of his mom's recipes (with her permission, of course) for this cookbook. According to Jeremy, Mrs. Noye developed a yogurt cookie for her dieting husband as a reward for staying on his diet. The cookie became a favorite of everyone in the family—probably because they are not really diet food.

I confess I usually don't like the flavor of a cooked banana, but in this recipe it adds moisture and sweetness and a subtle flavor that beautifully complements the raisins. Another confession: I'm not crazy about yogurt either. In this case, however, the tartness of the yogurt is the perfect foil for the soft, sweet cookie.

The Chocolate Banana Raisin Yogurt Cookies will keep for 3 to 4 days if stored in a tightly sealed plastic container. For long-term storage, 2 to 3 weeks, the cookies may be frozen in a tightly sealed plastic container to prevent dehydration and to protect them from freezer odors.

FRANNY'S BIG BOTTOM PIES

Yields 1 dozen 4-inch pies

INGREDIENTS

BIG BOTTOM COCOA COOKIE BATTER

2	cups all-purpose flour
½	cup unsweetened cocoa powder
½	teaspoon salt
1	cup granulated sugar
4	tablespoons unsalted butter
1	large egg
1	teaspoon pure vanilla extract
½	cup hot water
1	teaspoon baking soda
½	cup nonfat buttermilk
8	ounces semisweet chocolate mini-morsels

FRANNY'S FILLING

½	pound unsalted butter, cut into 1-ounce pieces
1	tablespoon pure vanilla extract
4	cups confectioners' sugar
8	ounces semisweet chocolate mini-morsels

EQUIPMENT

Measuring cups, measuring spoons, cook's knife, cutting board, sifter, wax paper, table-model electric mixer with paddle, rubber spatula, 1-quart bowl, whisk, instant-read test thermometer, 4 nonstick baking sheets, plastic wrap, plastic cookie storage container with lid

MAKE THE BIG BOTTOM COOKIES

Preheat the oven to 375 degrees Fahrenheit.

In a sifter combine the flour, cocoa powder, and salt. Sift onto a large piece of wax paper and set aside until needed.

Place the granulated sugar and 4 tablespoons butter in the bowl of an electric mixer fitted with a paddle. Beat on medium for 3 minutes until smooth. Use a rubber spatula to scrape down the sides of the bowl, then continue to beat on medium for 2 more minutes until very smooth. Scrape down the bowl once again. Add the egg and 1 teaspoon vanilla extract and beat on medium for 30 seconds. Scrape down the bowl. In a 1-quart bowl, whisk together the hot water (about 110 degrees Fahrenheit) and the baking soda. Set aside for a few seconds. Operate the mixer on low while first gradually adding the sifted dry ingredients, then the buttermilk, followed by the hot-water-and-baking-soda mixture. Mix until incorporated, about 1 minute. Stop the mixer, add 8 ounces chocolate mini-morsels, and mix on medium for 30 seconds. Remove the bowl from the mixer and use a rubber spatula to finish mixing the batter until thoroughly combined.

Using a large heaping tablespoon of batter (approximately 1½ ounces) for each cookie, portion 6 cookies, evenly spaced, onto each of 4 nonstick baking sheets. Place the baking sheets on the top and center racks of the preheated oven and bake for 10 minutes until the tops no longer appear wet, rotating the sheets from top to center halfway through the baking time (at that time also turn each sheet 180 degrees). Remove the cookies from the oven and cool on the baking sheets for 30 minutes.

PREPARE FRANNY'S FILLING

Place ½ pound butter in the bowl of an electric mixer fitted with a paddle. Beat on medium for 2 minutes. Use a rubber spatula to scrape down the sides of the bowl. Add 1 tablespoon vanilla extract and beat on high for 2 minutes until light. Operate the mixer on low while gradually adding the confectioners' sugar until incorporated, about 1 minute. Scrape down the sides of the bowl. Beat on high for 2 minutes until fluffy. Stop the mixer, add 8 ounces chocolate mini-morsels, and mix on medium for 30 seconds. Remove the bowl from the mixer and use a rubber spatula to finish mixing the filling until thoroughly combined.

ASSEMBLE THE BIG BOTTOM PIES

Invert half of the cookies onto wax paper. Portion 3 tablespoons (approximately 2½ ounces) of Franny's Filling onto each inverted cookie half. Place the remaining cookies right-side-up (or should I say, bottom-side-down) onto the filling. Gently but firmly press down on the top cookie to spread the filling to the edges. Serve immediately, or individually wrap in plastic wrap and store in a tightly sealed plastic container.

THE CHEF'S TOUCH

My friend and electronic media agent, Simon Green, contributed the inspiration for Franny's Big Bottom Pies. Like many students who learn that you can't burn the candle at both ends on vegetables alone, Simon indulged himself with sweets as an undergraduate at Vassar. Simon was particularly smitten by Moon Pies, which a classmate of his periodically had flown in from Texas. Convinced that similar products with different names found in other parts of the world just aren't the same, Simon seeks out Moon Pies whenever he travels down South. Simon challenged me to come up with a version of his beloved Moon Pies, and even suggested the name. What I want to know is, who is Franny?

Franny's Big Bottom Pies will keep for a day or two at room temperature if stored in a tightly sealed plastic container. For long-term storage, 2 to 3 weeks, the pies may be frozen in a tightly sealed plastic container to prevent dehydration and to protect them from freezer odors. Thaw the pies before serving.

KELLY'S CHOCOLATE PISTACHIO COOKIES
Yields (in a perfect world) 4 dozen 3×2-inch cookies

INGREDIENTS

CHOCOLATE PISTACHIO COOKIE DOUGH

4½   cups all-purpose flour
½   teaspoon salt
1   pound unsalted butter, cut into 1-ounce pieces
1½   cups sour cream
3   large egg yolks
3   tablespoons water
3   tablespoons granulated sugar

CHOCOLATE PISTACHIO FILLING

¾   cup shelled unsalted pistachios
8   ounces semisweet chocolate, chopped into 1/4-inch pieces
1   cup granulated sugar
½   teaspoon ground cinnamon

EQUIPMENT

Measuring cups, measuring spoons, cook's knife, cutting board, sifter, wax paper, table-model electric mixer with paddle, 1-quart bowl, whisk, rubber spatula, plastic wrap, 4 baking sheets, food processor with metal blade, parchment paper, rolling pin, pizza cutter, pastry brush, plastic cookie storage container with lid

MAKE THE COOKIE DOUGH

In a sifter combine 4 cups flour and the salt. Sift onto a large piece of wax paper, then transfer to the bowl of an electric mixer fitted with a paddle. Add the butter and beat on low for 2 minutes until the butter is blended into the flour. In a 1-quart bowl whisk together the sour cream and 2 egg yolks, then add to the flour-and-butter mixture and beat on medium for 1 minute until combined. Remove the bowl from the mixer and use a rubber spatula to finish mixing the dough until thoroughly combined. Transfer the dough to a clean, dry cutting board and divide into 4 equal portions. Wrap each portion in plastic wrap and refrigerate for 1 hour.

MAKE THE CHOCOLATE PISTACHIO FILLING

Preheat the oven to 350 degrees Fahrenheit.

Toast the pistachios on a baking sheet in the preheated oven for 10 minutes. Cool the nuts to room temperature.

Place the semisweet chocolate, 1 cup sugar, pistachios, and ground cinnamon in the bowl of a food processor fitted with a metal blade. Pulse until the chocolate and nuts are finely chopped, about 15 seconds. Set aside.

ASSEMBLE AND BAKE THE COOKIES

Preheat the oven to 350 degrees Fahrenheit.

Line 4 baking sheets with parchment paper.

Remove 1 piece of the dough from the refrigerator. Remove and discard the plastic wrap. Place the dough on a clean, dry, well-floured work surface (the dough is sticky). Roll the dough into a rectangle approximately 12 inches long and 8 inches wide. Trim the edges to form an even rectangle 12 inches long and 8 inches wide. Sprinkle ¼ of the filling mixture (about ¾ cup) over the entire surface of the dough.

Use a pizza cutter to make 5 cuts across the width of the dough at 2-inch intervals (this will give you 6 2-inch-wide strips), then diagonally cut each strip in half lengthwise from corner to corner (this will give you 12 12-inch-long triangles that are each 2 inches wide at the base). Roll each triangle from the base to the point (flouring your fingertips as necessary to prevent the dough from sticking). Place the 12 portions evenly spaced on a parchment-lined baking sheet. Repeat the procedure with the remaining 3 pieces of dough. In a 1-quart bowl, make an egg wash by whisking together the remaining egg yolk and 3 tablespoons water until combined. Use a pastry brush to lightly brush each portion of rolled cookie dough with the egg wash. Lightly sprinkle the 3 tablespoons granulated sugar onto the cookies (make sure your hands are dry when you sprinkle or things could get sticky).

Place the baking sheets on the top and center racks of the preheated oven and bake for 24 minutes until lightly golden brown, rotating the sheets from top to center halfway through the baking time (at that time also turn each sheet 180 degrees). Remove the cookies from the oven and cool for 30 minutes. Store the cookies in a tightly sealed plastic container until ready to serve.

THE CHEF'S TOUCH

The Eastern European ancestry of Trellis Pastry Chef Kelly Bailey (née Seroczynski) makes her naturally adept in the production of rugelach, a traditional crescent-shaped cookie with a soft cream cheese dough. Working for a chocolate-obsessed person like me causes Kelly to push the chocolate envelope whenever she can. So here tradition meets obsession, and we end up with a tender bite of nirvana.

Take the time to shell your own pistachios. I have found that already-shelled pistachios lack flavor and are soft, neither of which improves after toasting. Although you can chop the pistachios and chocolate for the filling by hand, this is the sort of task that makes a food processor invaluable; hand-chopping with a cook's knife not only takes much longer, but the finished product will not be as fine.

This dough is tender and sticky. Please heed the directions and use plenty of flour when rolling the dough, and keep your fingers dry and well floured while handling the dough.

Kelly's Chocolate Pistachio Cookies will keep for 2 to 3 days at room temperature if stored in a tightly sealed plastic container. I have found that this delicious cookie does not do well when refrigerated or frozen. I recommend that you make only what will be consumed within 2 to 3 days.

For Kids at Heart

OPPOSITE: **White Chocolate Sunflower Cookies (see page 84)**   ABOVE: **Chocolate Malted Bars (see page 80)**

CHOCOLATE OATMEAL ROUNDUP COOKIES

Yields 3 dozen 3-inch cookies

THE CHEF'S TOUCH

This is about the only way I will eat oat-meal—in cookies. This healthful ingredient has a long history of feeding the masses, but I and many other fussy eaters will only consume oatmeal when it is swathed in (preferably chocolate) cookie dough.

Chocolate Oatmeal Roundup Cookies are designed for those lengthy stays out on the trail. They will keep for several days uncovered at room temperature, for several more days if stored at room temperature in a tightly sealed plastic container, and for two to three weeks when stored in the refrigerator. If you are planning for the millennium, freeze the cookies in a tightly sealed plastic container to prevent dehydration and to protect them from freezer odors.

INGREDIENTS

1	cup unsalted peanuts
2	cups all-purpose flour
¼	cup unsweetened cocoa powder
2	teaspoons baking powder
½	teaspoon salt
1	cup granulated sugar
1	cup tightly packed light brown sugar
¾	cup creamy peanut butter
½	pound unsalted butter, cut into 1-ounce pieces
2	large eggs
1	teaspoon pure vanilla extract
2	cups semisweet chocolate chips
1½	cups 100% natural quick oats

EQUIPMENT

Measuring cups, measuring spoons, cook's knife, cutting board, 3 nonstick baking sheets, sifter, wax paper, table-model electric mixer with paddle, rubber spatula, plastic cookie storage container with lid

MAKE THE COOKIES

Preheat the oven to 350 degrees Fahrenheit.

Toast the peanuts on a baking sheet in the preheated oven for 10 to 12 minutes until golden brown. Cool the nuts to room temperature before chopping with a cook's knife into ⅛-inch pieces.

In a sifter combine the flour, cocoa powder, baking powder, and salt. Sift onto a large piece of wax paper and set aside until needed.

Place the granulated sugar, light brown sugar, peanut butter, and butter in the bowl of an electric mixer fitted with a paddle. Beat on medium for 4 minutes until soft. Use a rubber spatula to scrape down the sides of the bowl, then beat on high for 2 minutes until fairly smooth. Add the eggs and vanilla extract and beat on medium for 1 minute until incorporated. Scrape down the bowl. Beat on high for 1 minute until smooth. Operate the mixer on low speed while gradually adding first the sifted dry ingredients, then the chocolate chips, oats, and chopped peanuts; mix until combined, about 1 minute. Remove the bowl from the mixer and use a rubber spatula to finish mixing the ingredients until thoroughly combined.

Using 2 heaping tablespoons of dough for each cookie (approximately 2 ounces), portion 12 cookies, evenly spaced, onto each of 3 nonstick baking sheets. Use your fingers (it's not a sticky dough) to gently press and slightly flatten each portion of dough into a disk 3 inches in diameter and ¾ inch thick. Place the baking sheets on the top and center racks of the preheated oven and bake for 18 to 20 minutes, rotating the sheets from top to center halfway through the baking time (at that time also turn each sheet 180 degrees). Remove the cookies from the oven and cool to room temperature on the baking sheets, about 30 minutes. Store the cooled cookies in a tightly sealed plastic container.

CHOCOLATE PEANUT BUTTER BENGAL COOKIES

Yields 4 dozen 2¼-inch cookies

INGREDIENTS

CHOCOLATE PEANUT BUTTER COOKIE BATTER

1   cup unsalted peanuts
6   ounces semisweet chocolate, chopped into ¼-inch pieces
1   cup creamy peanut butter
¾   cup granulated sugar
¼   pound unsalted butter, cut into 1-ounce pieces
1   large egg
2   teaspoons pure vanilla extract
1¼ cups all-purpose flour
⅛   teaspoon salt

CREAMY TOPPING

1¼ cups creamy peanut butter
¼   cup confectioners' sugar

CHOCOLATE DRIZZLE

8   ounces semisweet chocolate, chopped into ¼-inch pieces

EQUIPMENT

Measuring cups, cook's knife, cutting board, measuring spoons, 4 nonstick baking sheets, food processor with metal blade, double boiler, rubber spatula, 1-quart bowl, table-model electric mixer with paddle, plastic wrap, wax paper, plastic cookie storage container with lid

MAKE THE COOKIES

Preheat the oven to 325 degrees Fahrenheit.

Toast the peanuts on a baking sheet in the preheated oven for 10 to 12 minutes until golden brown. Cool the nuts to room temperature before finely chopping in a food processor fitted with a metal blade (about 20 seconds) or by hand with a cook's knife.

Heat 1 inch of water in the bottom half of a double boiler over medium heat. With the heat on, place 6 ounces semisweet chocolate in the top half of the double boiler. Use a rubber spatula to stir the chocolate until completely melted and smooth, about 4 to 6 minutes. Transfer the melted chocolate to a 1-quart bowl and set aside until needed.

Place 1 cup peanut butter, granulated sugar, and butter in the bowl of an electric mixer fitted with a paddle. Beat on medium for 2 minutes until soft. Use a rubber spatula to scrape down the sides of the bowl. Add the egg and the vanilla extract and beat on high for 3 minutes until smooth. Scrape down the sides of the bowl. Add the melted chocolate and the chopped peanuts and mix on medium until incorporated, about 1 minute. Operate the mixer on low while gradually adding the flour and the salt. Once the dry ingredients have been incorporated, about 30 seconds, remove the bowl from the mixer and use a rubber spatula to finish mixing the ingredients until thoroughly combined. Transfer the dough to a cutting board.

Divide the dough into 2 equal portions. With both palms, roll each portion of dough on a clean, dry cutting board to form each portion into a cylinder that is 12 inches long and 1½ inches in diameter. Individually wrap each portion in plastic wrap and place them in the refrigerator for 3 to 4 hours, until the dough is very firm to the touch.

Remove the dough from the refrigerator and discard the plastic wrap. Cut each piece of dough into 24 individual ½-inch-thick slices. Divide the slices onto 4 nonstick baking sheets, 12 evenly spaced slices per sheet. Place the baking sheets on the top and center racks of the preheated oven and bake for 16 to 18 minutes, rotating the sheets from top to center halfway through the baking time (at that time also turn each sheet 180 degrees). Remove the cookies from the oven and cool to room temperature on the baking sheets, about 30 minutes.

PREPARE THE CREAMY TOPPING

Place 1¼ cups peanut butter and the confectioners' sugar in the bowl of an electric mixer fitted with a paddle. Mix on low speed for 30 seconds. Use a rubber spatula to scrape down the sides of the bowl, then beat on high for 1 minute. Remove the bowl from the mixer and use a rubber spatula to finish mixing the ingredients until completely smooth. Set the topping as far out of reach as possible (the temptation to sample this treat is too great to risk) while making the chocolate drizzle.

MAKE THE CHOCOLATE DRIZZLE

Heat 1 inch of water in the bottom half of a double boiler over medium heat. With the heat on, place 8 ounces semisweet chocolate in the top half of the double boiler. Use a rubber spatula to stir the chocolate until completely melted and smooth, about 4 to 6 minutes. Transfer the melted chocolate to a 1-quart bowl and set aside until needed.

ASSEMBLE THE BENGALS

Place a heaping teaspoon of creamy topping in the center of each cookie. Use a small spatula or butter knife to spread the topping evenly over the top of each cookie.

Arrange the cookies close together on a piece of wax paper or parchment paper. Use a teaspoon to drizzle thin lines of melted chocolate onto the top of each cookie (relax and be fluid with the drizzle). Keep the cookies at room temperature for 25 to 30 minutes to firm the chocolate. Store the cookies in a tightly sealed plastic container until ready to serve.

THE CHEF'S TOUCH

Pile all of your favorite memories into one bowl and you have the recipe for this cookie. Chocolate, peanuts, and creamy peanut butter, topped with more of the same. If the mere thought of these ingredients doesn't evoke a smile, I suggest you start baking some Bengals immediately.

Chocolate Peanut Butter Bengals will keep for several days at room temperature if stored in a tightly sealed plastic container. They will also keep for more than a week covered with plastic wrap in the refrigerator. For long-term storage, up to several weeks, these cookies may be frozen. Freeze cookies in a tightly sealed plastic container to prevent dehydration and to protect them from freezer odors.

Drizzle thin lines of melted chocolate onto the top of each cookie.

BLACK MAGIC COOKIES WITH BLACKSTRAP ICING

Yields 4 dozen 2-inch cookies

INGREDIENTS

BLACK MAGIC COOKIE BATTER

1	cup raisins
¼	cup dark rum
3	cups all-purpose flour
¼	cup unsweetened cocoa powder
2	teaspoons baking powder
½	teaspoon ground allspice
½	teaspoon ground cinnamon
⅛	teaspoon salt
8	ounces semisweet chocolate, chopped into ¼-inch pieces
½	pound unsalted butter, cut into 1-ounce pieces
1	cup tightly packed light brown sugar
3	large eggs
1	teaspoon pure vanilla extract

BLACKSTRAP ICING

6	ounces semisweet chocolate, chopped into ¼-inch pieces
¾	cup heavy cream
¼	pound unsalted butter, cut into 1-ounce pieces
2	tablespoons blackstrap molasses

EQUIPMENT

Measuring cups, measuring spoons, cook's knife, cutting board, 1-quart plastic container with tight-fitting lid, sifter, wax paper, double boiler, rubber spatula, 1-quart bowl, table-model electric mixer with paddle, 4 nonstick baking sheets, 3-quart bowl, 1½-quart saucepan, plastic cookie storage container with lid

WEAVE THAT OLD BLACK MAGIC

Combine the raisins and the rum in a plastic container with a tight-fitting lid and steep at room temperature for 6 hours or overnight (don't reveal the location to the members of your household).

MAKE THE COOKIES

Preheat the oven to 350 degrees Fahrenheit.

In a sifter combine the flour, cocoa powder, baking powder, allspice, cinnamon, and salt. Sift onto a large piece of wax paper and set aside until needed.

Heat 1 inch of water in the bottom half of a double boiler over medium heat. With the heat on, place 8 ounces semisweet chocolate in the top half of the double boiler. Use a rubber spatula to stir the chocolate until completely melted and smooth, about 3 minutes. Transfer the melted chocolate to a 1-quart bowl and set aside until needed.

Combine ½ pound butter and the brown sugar in the bowl of an electric mixer fitted with a paddle. Beat on medium for 4 minutes until soft. Use a rubber spatula to scrape down the sides of the bowl. Continue to beat on medium for 4 more minutes until fairly smooth. Scrape down the bowl, then beat on high for 2 minutes until smooth. Add the eggs, one at a time, beating on medium for 1 minute and scraping down the sides of the bowl after each addition. Add the vanilla extract and beat on high for 1 minute. Scrape down the bowl. Add the melted chocolate and beat on medium for 30 seconds until incorporated. Add the rum-infused raisins and mix on low for 30 seconds until combined. Scrape down the bowl. Operate the mixer on low while gradually adding the sifted dry ingredients. When all the dry ingredients have been incorporated, about 1 minute, remove the bowl from the mixer and use a rubber spatula to finish mixing the dough until thoroughly combined.

Using a heaping tablespoon of dough for each cookie (approximately 1 ounce), portion 12 cookies, evenly spaced, onto each of 4 nonstick baking sheets. Place the baking sheets on the top and center racks of the preheated oven and bake for 10 to 12 minutes, rotating the sheets from top to center about halfway through the baking time (at that time also turn each sheet 180 degrees). Remove the cookies from the oven and cool to room temperature on the baking sheets, about 30 minutes.

MAKE THE BLACKSTRAP ICING

Place 6 ounces semisweet chocolate in a 3-quart bowl.

Heat the heavy cream, ¼ pound butter, and molasses in a 1½-quart saucepan over medium heat. Stir to dissolve the molasses, then bring to a boil. Pour the boiling cream mixture over the chocolate and set aside for 5 minutes. Stir until smooth. Keep the icing at room temperature for 1 hour before using.

Ice the cookies by spooning approximately 1 tablespoon of the icing onto the top of each cookie. Store the cookies in a tightly sealed plastic container until ready to serve.

CHOCOLATE ALMOND TRUFFLE BARS
Yields 4 dozen 1-inch bars

TRUFFLE BAR BATTER

2¾ cups sliced almonds
½   pound unsalted butter, cut into 1-ounce pieces, plus 2 tablespoons (melted)
1   pound semisweet chocolate, chopped into ¼-inch pieces
4   large eggs
6   large egg yolks
1   cup granulated sugar

ALMOND ICING

1½ cups sliced almonds
½   pound unsalted butter, cut into 1-ounce pieces
3   cups confectioners' sugar
1   teaspoon pure vanilla extract

EQUIPMENT

Measuring cups, cook's knife, cutting board, small nonstick saucepan, measuring spoons, baking sheet with sides, food processor with metal blade, 3-quart bowl, 9×13×2-inch nonstick rectangular baking pan, double boiler, rubber spatula, table-model electric mixer with paddle, toothpick, cake spatula, serrated knife with rounded tip, plastic cookie storage container with lid

MAKE THE TRUFFLE BAR

Preheat the oven to 325 degrees Fahrenheit.

Toast 2¾ cups sliced almonds on a baking sheet with sides in the preheated oven until lightly golden brown, about 10 minutes. Cool the almonds to room temperature before finely chopping for 10 seconds in a food processor fitted with a metal blade (you may also finely chop the almonds by hand using a cook's knife).

Place the finely chopped toasted almonds in a 3-quart bowl. Combine the almonds with 2 tablespoons melted butter. Mix by hand until the almonds bind together. Transfer the nut mixture to a 9×13×2-inch nonstick baking pan. Use your fingertips to press the almond mixture onto the bottom and into the corners and sides of the pan, creating an even layer. Set aside.

Heat 1 inch of water in the bottom half of a double boiler over medium heat. With the heat on, place the semisweet chocolate and ½ pound butter in the top half of the double boiler. Use a rubber spatula to stir the chocolate and butter until completely melted and smooth, about 10 minutes. Transfer the melted chocolate mixture to a bowl and set aside until needed.

Place the eggs, egg yolks, and granulated sugar in the bowl of an electric mixer fitted with a paddle. Beat on medium speed for 4 minutes. Use a rubber spatula to scrape down the sides of the bowl, then beat on high speed until slightly thickened and lemon-colored, about 3 minutes. Add the melted chocolate mixture and mix on low speed until incorporated, about 1 minute. Remove the bowl from the mixer and use a rubber spatula to finish mixing the batter until thoroughly combined.

Pour the batter over the almond mixture in the baking pan. Bake on the center rack of the preheated oven for 45 minutes until a toothpick inserted in the center comes out almost clean (a scant amount of baked batter will adhere to the toothpick). Remove the pan from the oven and cool at room temperature for 1 hour.

MAKE THE ALMOND ICING

Preheat the oven to 325 degrees Fahrenheit.

Toast 1½ cups sliced almonds on a baking sheet with sides in the preheated oven until lightly golden brown, about 10 minutes. Cool the almonds to room temperature before finely chopping for 10 seconds in a food processor fitted with a metal blade (you may also finely chop the almonds by hand using a cook's knife). Set aside.

Place ½ pound butter in the bowl of an electric mixer fitted with a paddle. Beat on medium until light, about 4 minutes. Operate the mixer on low speed while slowly adding the confectioners' sugar until incorporated, about 2 minutes. Scrape down the sides of the bowl. Add the vanilla extract and beat on high for 1 minute. Remove the bowl from the mixer and use a rubber spatula to finish mixing the icing until smooth (it will probably be so smooth you could spread it with a paper spatula). Spread 2 cups of the icing onto the top of the cooled Truffle Bar, spreading evenly to the edges. Add 1 cup finely chopped almonds to the remaining icing and use a rubber spatula to thoroughly combine. Spread the almond studded icing over the first layer of icing on the Truffle Bar.

TO SERVE

Use a serrated knife with a rounded tip to cut the Chocolate Almond Truffle Bar into 24 2-inch squares, then cut each square in half for 48 bars. For a clean cut, heat the blade of the knife under hot running water and wipe the blade dry before making each cut. Serve immediately or store for up to 2 days in a tightly sealed plastic container.

THE CHEF'S TOUCH

If this Chocolate Almond Truffle Bar doesn't rev up your pulse, then you may need to have your vital signs checked. Dense, intense layers embellished with almond icing make eating this bar cookie akin to walking on the moon.

To achieve the desired volume in the icing, an electric table-model or hand-held mixer is needed.

Chocolate Almond Truffle Bars are best served at room temperature and within a couple of days. If longer storage is desired, the bars may be refrigerated for several days, but bring the refrigerated bars to room temperature before serving. Do not return uneaten bars (I can't imagine there would be any) to the refrigerator.

If you are planning a large event and would like to serve bite-size portions, then you may halve each bar. This will give you 96 mini-bars.

PAISLEY BROWNIES
Yields 2 dozen 2-inch brownies

INGREDIENTS

1 10-ounce package frozen whole red raspberries in light syrup, thawed

1½ cups all-purpose flour

1 teaspoon baking powder

1 teaspoon salt

6 ounces white chocolate, chopped into ¼-inch pieces

12 ounces unsalted butter, cut into 1-ounce pieces

10 ounces semisweet chocolate, chopped into ¼-inch pieces

5 large eggs

1¼ cups granulated sugar

1 teaspoon pure vanilla extract

½ cup sour cream

EQUIPMENT

Measuring cups, measuring spoons, cook's knife, cutting board, food processor with metal blade, fine gauge strainer, rubber spatula, 4 5-quart bowls, sifter, wax paper, double boiler, table-model electric mixer with balloon whip, 9×13×2-inch nonstick rectangular baking pan, paring knife, toothpick, serrated knife with rounded tip, plastic cookie storage container with lid

THE CHEF'S TOUCH

The swirling of the batters should create an attractive and colorful paisley look. If you over-swirl, the brownies will have a less defined look but will still be quite delicious.

Paisley Brownies will keep for several days if stored in a tightly sealed plastic container in the refrigerator. Serve the brownies directly from the refrigerator.

MAKE THE PAISLEY BROWNIES

Preheat the oven to 300 degrees Fahrenheit.

Place the raspberries in the bowl of a food processor fitted with a metal blade. Pulse until liquefied, about 1 minute. Strain the raspberries through a fine strainer into a 5-quart bowl, using a rubber spatula to press down on the seeds to extract as much puree as possible (about ¾ cup puree). Discard the seeds. Set the puree aside until needed.

In a sifter combine the flour, baking powder, and salt. Sift onto a large piece of wax paper and set aside until needed.

Heat 1 inch of water in the bottom half of a double boiler over medium heat. Place the white chocolate and 4 ounces of butter in the top half. Use a rubber spatula to stir the chocolate and butter until completely melted and smooth, about 5 minutes. Transfer the melted white chocolate and butter to an empty 5-quart bowl and set aside until needed.

Again heat 1 inch of water in the bottom half of a double boiler over medium heat. Place the semisweet chocolate and the remaining 8 ounces of butter in the top half of the double boiler. Use a rubber spatula to stir the chocolate and butter until completely melted and smooth, about 7 minutes. Transfer the melted semisweet chocolate and butter to an empty 5-quart bowl and set aside until needed.

Place the eggs, sugar, and vanilla extract in the bowl of an electric mixer fitted with a balloon whip. Whisk on high for 2 minutes until soft. Use a rubber spatula to scrape down the sides of the bowl, then whisk on high for 4 minutes until slightly thickened and lemon-colored. Operate the mixer on low while gradually adding the sifted dry ingredients until incorporated, about 30 seconds. Remove the bowl from the mixer and add the sour cream. Use a rubber spatula to mix the ingredients until thoroughly combined.

Portion 2 cups of the batter into the bowl containing the pureed raspberries and stir until smooth. Portion 1 cup of the batter into the bowl containing the melted white chocolate mixture and stir until smooth. Portion the remaining 2 cups of batter into the bowl containing the melted semisweet chocolate mixture and stir until smooth. Pour the dark chocolate batter into a 9×13×2-inch nonstick baking pan and spread evenly over the bottom. Pour the white chocolate batter onto the top of the dark chocolate batter in swirls. Pour the raspberry batter over the other two batters in the same manner. Use the blade of a paring knife to swirl the batters together in a fanciful pattern (you should be having fun doing this). Bake on the center rack of the preheated oven until a toothpick inserted in the center comes out clean, about 1 hour and 10 minutes. Remove the brownies from the oven and allow to cool in the pan at room temperature for 1 hour.

Use a serrated knife with rounded tip to cut the brownies into 24 2-inch squares. For a clean cut, heat the blade of the knife under hot running water and wipe the blade dry before making each cut. Refrigerate the brownies for 2 to 3 hours before serving.

CHOCOLATE PRETZELS
Yields 2 dozen 3-inch cookies

4 ounces semisweet chocolate, chopped into ¼-inch pieces

¾ cup granulated sugar

½ pound unsalted butter, cut into 1-ounce pieces

2 tablespoons barley malt

3 large eggs

4¼ cups all-purpose flour

4 tablespoons heavy cream

4 tablespoons turbinado sugar

EQUIPMENT

Cook's knife, cutting board, measuring cups, measuring spoons, double boiler, rubber spatula, 1-quart bowl, table-model electric mixer with paddle, wax paper, 2 nonstick baking sheets, pastry brush, plastic cookie storage container with lid

MAKE THE PRETZELS

Preheat the oven to 350 degrees Fahrenheit.

Heat 1 inch of water in the bottom half of a double boiler over medium heat. With the heat on, place the semisweet chocolate in the top half of the double boiler. Use a rubber spatula to stir the chocolate until completely melted and smooth, about 3 minutes. Transfer the melted chocolate to a 1-quart bowl and set aside until needed.

Place the granulated sugar, butter, and barley malt in the bowl of an electric mixer fitted with a paddle. Beat on medium for 4 minutes until fairly smooth. Use a rubber spatula to scrape down the sides of the bowl, then beat on high for 1 minute until smooth. Add the eggs, one at a time, beating on medium for 1 minute and scraping down the sides of the bowl after each addition. Add the melted chocolate and mix on low until incorporated, about 30 seconds. Operate the mixer on low while gradually adding 3¾ cups flour until incorporated, about 1 minute. Remove the bowl from the mixer and use a rubber spatula to finish mixing the dough until thoroughly combined.

Portion the dough into 24 heaping tablespoons (approximately 1¾ ounces each) onto a large piece of wax paper. On a clean, dry surface, roll each portion of dough (using the remaining ½ cup of flour as necessary to prevent the dough from sticking) into a rope 10 inches long and ½ inch in diameter. Form each into a pretzel shape, then transfer onto 2 nonstick baking sheets, 12 evenly spaced pretzels per baking sheet.

Brush each pretzel dough portion lightly with heavy cream and sprinkle evenly and lightly with turbinado sugar. Place the baking sheets on the top and center racks of the preheated oven and bake for 25 minutes until lightly browned, rotating the sheets from top to center halfway through the baking time (at that time also turn each sheet 180 degrees). Remove from the oven and cool to room temperature on the baking sheets, about 30 minutes. Store the cooled pretzels in a tightly sealed plastic container.

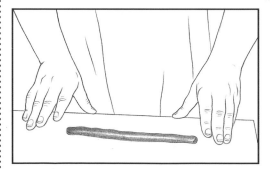

Roll each portion of dough into a rope 10 inches long and 1/2 inch in diameter.

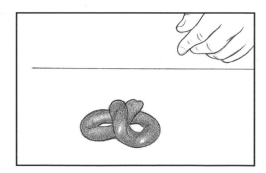

Form each elongated portion into a pretzel shape.

THE CHEF'S TOUCH

Many people enjoy chocolate-dipped traditional pretzels, and now we have made a good thing even better. Here the shape may be conventional, but we added a flavor twist of barley malt to the sweet dough.

Barley malt, commonly associated with brewing and distilling, lends a distinct flavor to this cookie. Look for barley malt in the health-food section at the supermarket.

Turbinado sugar can be purchased under the brand name of Sugar in the Raw. This sugar has only been partially refined, leaving it with an attractively different light brown color.

Chocolate Pretzels will keep for several days at room temperature if stored in a tightly sealed plastic container. For long-term storage, up to several weeks, the pretzels may be frozen. Freeze the pretzels in a tightly sealed plastic container to prevent dehydration and to protect them from freezer odors.

Consider serving ramekins of fresh fruit purees to accompany the pretzels.

MONKEY BARS
Yields 4 dozen 1-inch bars

INGREDIENTS

MONKEY BAR BATTER

1   cup walnut pieces
1   cup all-purpose flour
½   teaspoon baking powder
½   teaspoon salt
½   pound unsalted butter, cut into 1-ounce pieces
1   cup granulated sugar
3   large eggs
1   teaspoon pure vanilla extract
2   pounds medium-size ripe bananas, peeled
2   cups semisweet chocolate chips

MONKEY BAR ICING

1   cup heavy cream
4   tablespoons granulated sugar
4   ounces semisweet chocolate, chopped into ¼-inch pieces
4   ounces unsweetened chocolate, chopped into ¼-inch pieces

EQUIPMENT

Measuring cups, measuring spoons, cook's knife, cutting board, baking sheet, sifter, wax paper, table-model electric mixer with paddle, rubber spatula, 9×13×2-inch nonstick rectangular baking pan, 1½-quart saucepan, 3-quart bowl, whisk, cake spatula, serrated knife with rounded tip, plastic cookie storage container with lid

MAKE THE MONKEY BARS

Preheat the oven to 325 degrees Fahrenheit.

Toast the walnuts on a baking sheet in the preheated oven for 7 minutes. Remove the nuts from the oven and set aside to cool at room temperature until needed.

In a sifter combine the flour, baking powder, and salt. Sift onto a large piece of wax paper and set aside until needed.

Place the butter and 1 cup sugar in the bowl of an electric mixer fitted with a paddle. Beat on medium speed for 2 minutes until soft. Use a rubber spatula to scrape down the sides of the bowl. Add the eggs, one at a time, beating on medium for 1 minute and scraping down the sides of the bowl after each addition. Add 1 teaspoon vanilla extract and beat on high for 1 minute. Add the whole peeled bananas (you can break them in half, but it really isn't necessary) and beat for 2 minutes on medium until fairly smooth. Scrape down the sides of the bowl. Operate the mixer on low while gradually adding the sifted dry ingredients until incorporated, about 1 minute. Add the chocolate chips and the toasted walnuts and mix on low to incorporate, about 20 seconds. Remove the bowl from the mixer and use a rubber spatula to finish mixing the ingredients until thoroughly combined.

Pour the batter into the 9×13×2-inch nonstick baking pan. Use a rubber spatula to spread the batter in an even layer. Bake on the center rack of the preheated oven for 40 minutes until golden brown around the edges and set in the center. Remove the pan from the oven and allow to stand at room temperature for 1 hour before making the icing.

MAKE THE MONKEY BAR ICING

Heat the heavy cream and 4 tablespoons sugar in a 1½-quart saucepan over medium-high heat. When hot, stir to dissolve the sugar. Bring to a boil. Place the semisweet chocolate and unsweetened chocolate in a 3-quart bowl. Pour the boiling cream over the chocolate and stir with a whisk until smooth.

Pour the icing over the cooled Monkey Bar. Use a cake spatula to spread the icing evenly over the entire surface of the bar. Refrigerate for 1 hour before serving.

TO SERVE

Use a serrated knife with rounded tip to cut the Monkey Bars into 24 2-inch squares, then cut each square in half to yield 48 bars. For a clean cut, heat the blade of the knife under hot running water and wipe the blade dry before making each cut. Serve immediately or store in a tightly sealed plastic container until you are ready to eat.

Monkey Bars may be served either chilled or at room temperature. The banana flavor is enhanced and the texture softens when the bars are served at room temperature, so you decide. Monkey Bars will keep for 2 to 3 days at room temperature if stored in a tightly sealed plastic container. When refrigerated in a similar container, the bars will keep for several days.

If you are a banana fanatic—and who isn't—try serving these delicious bars with a scoop or two of the Banana Split Ice Cream (see page 114). Now there's a combo that will have you swinging.

SUCCESSIVELY EXCESSIVELY CRUNCHY PEANUT BUTTER BROWNIES

Yields 2 dozen 2-inch brownies

INGREDIENTS

EXCESSIVELY CRUNCHY PEANUT BUTTER BROWNIE BATTER

1½ cups unsalted peanuts

1½ cups all-purpose flour

1½ teaspoons baking powder

1 teaspoon salt

1¼ cups tightly packed light brown sugar

1 cup creamy peanut butter

¼ pound unsalted butter, cut into 1-ounce pieces

¼ cup dark corn syrup

4 large eggs

1 teaspoon pure vanilla extract

SUCCESSIVELY EXCESSIVE TOPPING

¾ cup heavy cream

6 ounces semisweet chocolate, chopped into ¼-inch pieces

1 cup semisweet chocolate chips

1 cup peanut butter chips

EQUIPMENT

Measuring cups, measuring spoons, cook's knife, cutting board, baking sheet, sifter, wax paper, table-model electric mixer with paddle, rubber spatula, 9 x 13 x 2-inch nonstick rectangular baking pan, toothpick, 1½-quart saucepan, 2 3-quart bowls, whisk, cake spatula, serrated knife with rounded tip, plastic cookie storage container with lid

MAKE THE BROWNIE TO EXCESS

Preheat the oven to 325 degrees Fahrenheit.

Toast the peanuts on a baking sheet in the preheated oven until golden brown, about 10 to 12 minutes. Cool the peanuts to room temperature before chopping by hand with a cook's knife into ¼-inch pieces. Set aside.

In a sifter combine the flour, baking powder, and salt. Sift onto a large piece of wax paper and set aside until needed.

Place the light brown sugar, peanut butter, unsalted butter, and the corn syrup in the bowl of an electric mixer fitted with a paddle. Beat on medium for 4 minutes. Use a rubber spatula to scrape down the sides of the bowl, then beat on medium for 2 more minutes. Scrape down the bowl. Add the eggs, one at a time, beating on medium for 1 minute and scraping down the sides of the bowl after each addition. Add the vanilla extract and beat on medium for 1 minute. Operate the mixer on low while gradually adding the sifted dry ingredients until incorporated, about 1 minute. Add ¾ cup chopped peanuts (the remaining peanuts are for the topping) and beat on medium for 10 seconds. Remove the bowl from the mixer and use a rubber spatula to finish mixing the ingredients until thoroughly combined.

Transfer the batter to a 9×13×2-inch nonstick baking pan. Use a rubber spatula to spread the batter in an even layer. Place the pan on the center rack of the preheated oven and bake for 35 minutes until a toothpick inserted in the center of the brownie comes out clean. Remove from the oven and allow to stand at room temperature for 1 hour before finishing with the Successively Excessive Topping.

PREPARE THE SUCCESSIVELY EXCESSIVE TOPPING

Heat the heavy cream in a 1½-quart saucepan over medium-high heat. Bring to a boil. Place the chopped semisweet chocolate in a 3-quart bowl. Pour the boiling cream over the chocolate and stir with a whisk until smooth. Congratulations—you have just created ganache!

Pour the ganache over the cooled brownie. Use a cake spatula to spread the ganache evenly over the entire surface of the brownie.

Combine in a 3-quart bowl the chocolate chips, peanut butter chips, and the remaining ¾ cup chopped unsalted peanuts.

Sprinkle the chips and nuts evenly over the ganache. Refrigerate the brownie for 1 hour before cutting. This will make the ganache layer firm enough to cut.

Use a serrated knife with rounded tip to cut the brownie into 24 2-inch squares. For a clean cut, heat the blade of the knife under hot running water and wipe the blade dry before making each cut. Serve immediately or store the brownies in a tightly sealed plastic container.

CHOCO COCOS

Yields 4 dozen 2½-inch cookies

THE CHEF'S TOUCH

Purchase two 1½-pound coconuts for this recipe. They may yield slightly more meat than required for this recipe, but two smaller coconuts or one larger one may not yield enough. Be certain to shake the coconut before purchasing to ensure that it has plenty of liquid (an indication of quality). Use a Phillips-head screwdriver or an ice pick to punch out two of the three coconut eyes, then pour out the coconut liquid. Use only the amount of coconut noted in the recipe (make yourself a piña colada with any leftovers).

To facilitate the harvesting of the coconut meat, I suggest cracking the "milked" coconuts in half by striking them a sharp blow with a hammer. Place the coconut halves, meat side up, on a baking sheet and bake in a preheated 300-degree-Fahrenheit oven for 30 minutes. Remove from the oven and cool to room temperature before handling. Use a large metal spoon to pry the coconut meat away from the hull. Use a sharp paring knife to peel the brownish skin away from the white meat.

For best results use a food processor fitted with a shredding disc when shredding coconut meat (it takes only seconds to shred 12 ounces' worth). The food processor will yield beautifully shredded coconut meat consistent in size and texture. Other equipment such as a hand-held box grater will produce results that are substantially less consistent.

The Cocos will keep for several days at room temperature if stored in a tightly sealed plastic container. For long-term storage, up to several weeks, the cookies may be frozen in a tightly sealed plastic container to prevent dehydration and to protect them from freezer odors.

INGREDIENTS

12 ounces fresh coconut, shredded

3½ cups all-purpose flour

1½ teaspoons baking powder

½ teaspoon baking soda

½ teaspoon salt

4 ounces unsweetened chocolate, chopped into ¼-ounce pieces

½ pound unsalted butter, cut into 1-ounce pieces

2 cups granulated sugar

2 large eggs

EQUIPMENT

Phillips-head screwdriver, hammer, large metal spoon, paring knife, food processor with #14 shredding disc, measuring cups, measuring spoons, cook's knife, cutting board, 4 nonstick baking sheets, sifter, wax paper, double boiler, rubber spatula, 1-quart bowl, table-model electric mixer with paddle, plastic cookie storage container with lid

MAKE THE CHOCO COCOS

Preheat the oven to 350 degrees Fahrenheit.

Spread the shredded coconut on a nonstick baking sheet in an even, thin layer. Toast the coconut in the preheated oven for 22 to 24 minutes until very lightly golden brown. Remove from the oven and transfer to a room temperature baking sheet (to prevent further toasting). After toasting, the weight of the coconut will be 6 ounces. Allow the coconut to cool to room temperature.

In a sifter combine the flour, baking powder, baking soda, and salt. Sift onto a large piece of wax paper and set aside until needed.

Heat 1 inch of water in the bottom half of a double boiler over medium heat. With the heat on, place the unsweetened chocolate in the top half of the double boiler. Use a rubber spatula to stir the chocolate until completely melted and smooth, about 3 minutes. Transfer the melted chocolate to a 1-quart bowl and set aside.

Place the butter and sugar in the bowl of an electric mixer fitted with a paddle. Beat on medium for 2 minutes until soft. Use a rubber spatula to scrape down the sides of the bowl, then beat on high for 4 minutes until smooth. Add the eggs and beat on medium for 2 minutes; scrape down the bowl. Add the melted chocolate and beat on medium speed for 30 seconds until incorporated. Operate the mixer on low while gradually adding the sifted dry ingredients. Once all the dry ingredients have been incorporated, about 30 seconds, remove the bowl from the mixer and use a rubber spatula to finish mixing the ingredients until thoroughly combined.

Using a heaping tablespoon of dough for each cookie (approximately 1 ounce), portion 12 cookies, evenly spaced, onto each of 4 nonstick baking sheets. Place 1 level tablespoon of toasted coconut (⅙ ounce) on each portion of cookie dough. Use your fingers to press down on each portion, forming a 2-inch-diameter, ¾-inch-thick disk from each

portion of coconut-topped dough. Place the baking sheets on the top and center racks of the preheated oven and bake for 10 minutes, rotating the sheets from top to center about halfway through the baking time (at that time also turn each sheet 180 degrees). Remove the cookies from the oven and allow to cool to room temperature on the baking sheets, about 30 minutes. Store the cooled cookies in a tightly sealed plastic container.

COCOA BROWNIES WITH COCOA MAPLE ICING

Yields 2 dozen 2-inch brownies

INGREDIENTS

COCOA BROWNIE BATTER

2 cups all-purpose flour
1 teaspoon baking soda
½ teaspoon salt
1½ cups tightly packed light brown
    sugar
½ cup sour cream
2 large eggs
1 teaspoon pure vanilla extract
½ pound unsalted butter, cut into
    1-ounce pieces
1 cup water
¼ cup unsweetened cocoa powder

COCOA MAPLE ICING

2 cups walnuts
2½ cups confectioners' sugar
¼ pound unsalted butter, cut into
    1-ounce pieces
¼ cup heavy cream
¼ cup pure maple syrup
¼ cup unsweetened cocoa powder

EQUIPMENT

Measuring cups, measuring spoons,
cook's knife, cutting board, sifter, 7-quart
bowl, 4-quart bowl, whisk, 1½-quart
saucepan, rubber spatula, 9×13×2-inch
nonstick rectangular baking pan, toothpick, baking sheet, food processor with
metal blade, serrated knife with rounded
tip, plastic cookie storage container
with lid

MAKE THE COCOA BROWNIES

Preheat the oven to 350 degrees Fahrenheit.

In a sifter combine the flour, baking soda, and salt. Sift into a 7-quart bowl and set aside until needed.

In a 4-quart bowl, whisk together the light brown sugar, sour cream, eggs, and vanilla extract until thoroughly combined.

Heat ½ pound butter with the water and ¼ cup cocoa powder in a 1½-quart saucepan over medium-high heat. Bring to a boil. Immediately pour the boiling mixture into the mixing bowl with the sifted dry ingredients, then add the egg-and–sour-cream mixture. Use a rubber spatula to stir the mixture (don't worry if it looks more like a mess than a marvel at this point) until thoroughly combined. Transfer the batter to a 9 x 13 x 2-inch nonstick baking pan. Use a rubber spatula to spread batter evenly over the bottom of the pan. Place the pan on the center rack of the preheated oven and bake until a toothpick inserted in the center comes out clean, about 24 minutes. Set pans aside while preparing the icing.

PREPARE THE COCOA MAPLE ICING

Preheat the oven to 350 degrees Fahrenheit.

Toast the walnuts on a baking sheet in the preheated oven for 8 minutes. Cool the walnuts to room temperature before finely chopping in a food processor fitted with a metal blade or by hand with a cook's knife.

Combine the confectioners' sugar and chopped walnuts in a 7-quart bowl.

Heat ¼ pound butter with the heavy cream, maple syrup, and ¼ cup cocoa powder in a 1½-quart saucepan over medium-high heat. Bring to a boil. Immediately pour the boiling mixture into the bowl with the confectioners' sugar and walnuts; whisk to combine.

Pour the icing over the baked Cocoa Brownie and spread evenly. Allow to stand at room temperature for 1 hour before cutting.

TO SERVE

Use a serrated knife with rounded tip to cut the Cocoa Brownie into 24 2-inch squares. For a clean cut, heat the blade of the knife under hot running water and wipe the blade dry before making each cut. Serve immediately or store the brownies in a tightly sealed plastic container.

THE CHEF'S TOUCH

With great authority, my seven-year-old niece Ellery told me that brownies are flat chocolate cake cut into squares. Brownies do come in a variety of textures: dense and chewy like fudge, crunchy and cookielike, and yes, even moist and cakelike. And there are actually brownies made without chocolate—horrors!—called blondies.

Our Cocoa Brownie With Cocoa Maple Icing is a cakelike version. The preparation for the brownie is a bit unconventional and the icing evolves more like a sauce than the traditional fluffy topping. The end result, however, is anything but odd. Rather, the moist and delicate brownie has a dense and shiny icing that could reflect your smile as you prepare to take a bite.

Maple syrup gives the icing a subtle undertone. It is important to achieve this wee bit of alchemy with pure maple syrup, not maple-flavored syrup.

Cocoa Brownies With Cocoa Maple Icing will keep for a couple of days at room temperature stored in a tightly sealed plastic container. For longer storage, 4 to 5 days, cover the brownies with plastic wrap or store in a tightly sealed plastic container and refrigerate.

CHOCOLATE MALTED BARS
Yields 4 dozen 1-inch bars

INGREDIENTS

¼ cup barley malt sweetener

2 tablespoons unsweetened cocoa powder

1 tablespoon cornstarch

6 large egg whites

⅛ teaspoon cream of tartar

⅛ teaspoon salt

1 cup confectioners' sugar

1 pound semisweet chocolate, chopped into ¼-inch pieces

2 ounces white chocolate, chopped into ¼-inch pieces

EQUIPMENT

Measuring cups, measuring spoons, cook's knife, cutting board, 2 10×15-inch baking sheets, parchment paper, sifter, wax paper, electric mixer with balloon whip, rubber spatula, large pastry bag, 7-quart bowl, double boiler, 9×13×2-inch nonstick rectangular baking pan, 1-quart bowl, teaspoon, serrated knife with rounded tip, plastic cookie storage container with lid

THE CHEF'S TOUCH

You can find barley malt sweetener at your local health food store. It is highly water absorbent, so be sure to store it in a tightly sealed plastic container.

See "Notes from Ganache Hill" (page 6) for purchasing information on white chocolate.

Chocolate Malted Bars will keep crunchy and delicious for several days stored in a tightly sealed plastic container in the refrigerator or a cool dry room.

Note: Photograph appears on page 59.

MAKE THE CHOCOLATE MALTED BARS

Preheat the oven to 200 degrees Fahrenheit.

Line 2 10×15-inch baking sheets with parchment paper. Set aside.

In a sifter combine the barley malt sweetener, cocoa powder, and corn starch. Sift onto a large piece of wax paper and set aside until needed.

Make a meringue by whisking the egg whites, cream of tartar, and salt on high in the bowl of an electric mixer fitted with a balloon whip. Whisk until soft peaks form, about 1 minute. Adjust speed to medium and continue to whisk while gradually adding the confectioners' sugar. Whisk until stiff, but not dry, about 3 minutes. Stop the mixer, add the sifted dry ingredients, and whisk 30 seconds on medium, just until incorporated. Remove the bowl from the mixer and use a rubber spatula to thoroughly combine the ingredients.

Fill a pastry bag (with no tip) with the meringue. Pipe 7 rows of meringue, each 1 inch wide, 14 inches long, and ¼ inch apart, onto each of the 2 parchment paper–lined baking sheets. Place the baking sheets in the preheated oven and bake the meringue strips for 2 hours. Remove the meringue from the oven and cool to room temperature for 30 minutes before handling.

Remove the meringue from the parchment paper-lined sheets and transfer to a cutting board. Use a cook's knife to cut the meringue strips into ½-inch pieces. Transfer the pieces to a 7-quart bowl. Set aside.

Heat 1 inch of water in the bottom half of a double boiler over medium heat. With the heat on, place the semisweet chocolate in the top half of the double boiler. Use a rubber spatula to stir the chocolate until completely melted and smooth, about 5 minutes. Pour the melted chocolate over the meringue pieces in the bowl. Use a rubber spatula to fold chocolate and meringue together, completely coating the meringue pieces with chocolate. Transfer the mixture to a 9×13×2-inch nonstick baking pan. Use a rubber spatula to spread evenly (but don't press down those crispy meringue chunks) over the bottom of the pan. Set aside at room temperature while melting the white chocolate.

Heat 1 inch of water in the bottom half of a double boiler over medium heat. With the heat on, place the white chocolate in the top half of the double boiler. Use a rubber spatula to stir the chocolate until completely melted and smooth, about 3 minutes. Transfer the melted chocolate to a 1-quart bowl. Use a teaspoon to drizzle the melted white chocolate over the entire surface of the chocolate meringue mixture, creating a variegated effect. Refrigerate for 1 hour before cutting.

Use a serrated knife with rounded tip to cut the Chocolate Malted Bars into 24 2-inch squares, then cut the squares in half for 48 bars. For a clean cut, heat the blade of the knife under hot running water and wipe the blade dry before making each cut. Serve immediately or store in a tightly sealed plastic container in the refrigerator.

CHOCOLATE BOULDERS

Yields 3 dozen 2½-inch cookies

INGREDIENTS

1½ cups pecan pieces
1 pound semisweet chocolate, 8 ounces chopped into ¼-inch pieces and 8 ounces chopped into ⅛-inch pieces
½ pound unsalted butter, cut into 1-ounce pieces
1 cup tightly packed light brown sugar
3 large eggs
1 teaspoon pure vanilla extract
3 cups all-purpose flour
1 teaspoon baking powder
1 teaspoon salt

EQUIPMENT

Measuring cups, cook's knife, cutting board, measuring spoons, 3 nonstick baking sheets, double boiler, rubber spatula, 1-quart bowl, table-model electric mixer with paddle, plastic cookie storage container with lid

THE CHEF'S TOUCH

If you love sweets but haven't put in many hours in the kitchen (and prefer to keep it that way), these cookies are for you. Chocolate Boulders are best eaten within a day or two of baking. In fact, they are at their best when served within a few hours of being removed from the oven.

MAKE THE BOULDERS

Preheat the oven to 350 degrees Fahrenheit.

Toast the pecans on a baking sheet in the preheated oven for 10 minutes. Remove the nuts from the oven and set aside to cool to room temperature before using.

Heat 1 inch of water in the bottom half of a double boiler over medium heat. With the heat on, place the ¼-inch pieces of chocolate in the top half of the double boiler. Use a rubber spatula to stir the chocolate until completely melted and smooth, about 4 to 6 minutes. Transfer the melted chocolate to a 1-quart bowl and set aside until needed.

Place the butter and brown sugar in the bowl of an electric mixer fitted with a paddle. Beat on medium speed for 3 minutes until soft. Use a rubber spatula to scrape down the sides of the bowl, then beat on high for 2 minutes until fairly smooth. Scrape down the bowl. Add the eggs and the vanilla extract and beat on medium for 3 minutes until smooth. Scrape down the bowl. Beat on high for 2 minutes until very smooth. Add the melted chocolate and beat on medium for 1 minute until incorporated. Operate the mixer on low speed while gradually adding the flour, baking soda, and salt and mix until incorporated, about 30 seconds. Stop the mixer and add the chocolate chopped into ⅛-inch pieces and the toasted pecans, and mix on low for 30 seconds. Remove the bowl from the mixer and use a rubber spatula to finish mixing the dough until thoroughly combined.

Using a heaping tablespoon of dough for each cookie (approximately 1¾ ounces), portion 12 cookies, evenly spaced, onto each of 3 nonstick baking sheets. Place the baking sheets on the top and center racks of the preheated oven and bake for 12 to 14 minutes, rotating the sheets from top to center halfway through the baking time (at that time also turn each sheet 180 degrees). Remove the cookies from the oven and cool to room temperature on the baking sheets, about 30 minutes. Store the cooled cookies in a tightly sealed plastic container.

WHITE CHOCOLATE PINEAPPLE UPSIDE-DOWN BARS

Yields 4 dozen 1-inch bars

EQUIPMENT
Measuring cups, cook's knife, cutting board, measuring spoons, baking sheet, 9 x 13 x 2-inch nonstick rectangular baking pan, sifter, wax paper, table-model electric mixer with paddle, rubber spatula, toothpick, serrated knife with rounded tip, plastic cookie storage container with lid

INGREDIENTS

1	cup pecans
½	pound dried pineapple slices, chopped into ¼-inch pieces
1	cup dried cherries
1½	cups all-purpose flour
2	teaspoons baking powder
½	teaspoon salt
1	cup tightly packed light brown sugar
6	ounces unsalted butter, cut into 1-ounce pieces
2	large eggs
1	teaspoon pure vanilla extract
4	ounces white chocolate, chopped into ¼-inch pieces

THE CHEF'S TOUCH

Like a grandfather with scores of grandchildren, I love all of my sweet recipes, but I can't help but have a favorite one or two—and the White Chocolate Pineapple Upside-Down Bar is at the top of my list. This delicious confection is just as delightful eaten midmorning as it is devoured late at night.

Look for the dried pineapples in the bulk foods section at your specialty grocer or upscale supermarket. The dried cherries, which are expensive, are usually located in the specialty food section or sometimes near baking-related items. You could substitute raisins for the cherries, but you will miss the color and the tasty zing that are special to the cherries.

See "Notes from Ganache Hill" (page 6) for purchasing information on white chocolate.

White Chocolate Pineapple Upside-Down Bars are best enjoyed within a day or two of baking. For a satisfying dessert, cut into large squares rather than bars and serve warm with a large dollop of whipped cream.

MAKE THE WHITE CHOCOLATE PINEAPPLE UPSIDE-DOWN BARS

Preheat the oven to 350 degrees Fahrenheit.

Toast the pecans on a baking sheet in the preheated oven for 5 to 6 minutes. Remove from the oven and cool to room temperature. Use a cook's knife to chop the pecans into ¼-inch pieces.

Sprinkle the pineapple pieces and the dried cherries in an even layer over the bottom of the 9×13×2-inch nonstick baking pan. Sprinkle the chopped pecans over the fruit in an even layer. Set aside until needed.

In a sifter combine the flour, baking powder, and salt. Sift onto a large piece of wax paper and set aside until needed.

Place the light brown sugar and the butter in the bowl of an electric mixer fitted with a paddle. Beat on medium for 4 minutes. Use a rubber spatula to scrape down the sides of the bowl, then continue to beat on medium for 4 more minutes. Scrape down the bowl. Add the eggs, one at a time, beating on medium for 1 minute and scraping down the sides of the bowl after each addition. Add the vanilla extract and beat on medium for 1 minute. Operate the mixer on low while gradually adding the sifted dry ingredients, followed by the chopped white chocolate; mix for 1 minute. Remove the bowl from the mixer and use a rubber spatula to finish mixing the batter until thoroughly combined.

Transfer the batter to the fruit-and-nut-layered pan. Use a rubber spatula to spread the batter evenly over the mixture. Bake on the center rack of the preheated oven until a toothpick inserted in the center comes out clean, about 35 minutes. Remove from the oven and cool to room temperature, about 1 hour.

Use a serrated knife with a rounded tip to cut the White Chocolate Pineapple Upside-Down Bar into 24 2-inch squares, then cut the squares in half for 48 bars. For a clean cut, heat the blade of the knife under hot running water and wipe the blade dry before making each cut. Serve the bars, bottom side up, immediately or store in a tightly sealed plastic container.

WHITE CHOCOLATE SUNFLOWER COOKIES
Yields 3 dozen 3-inch cookies

EQUIPMENT

Measuring cups, measuring spoons, cook's knife, cutting board, 4 nonstick baking sheets (1 with sides), sifter, wax paper, double boiler, rubber spatula, 1-quart bowl, table-model electric mixer with paddle, plastic cookie storage container with lid

THE CHEF'S TOUCH

American Indians were enamored of sunflowers. Native to North America, this showy annual was extensively cultivated by many tribes. Sunflower seeds, a good source of protein, were used in a variety of ways: to make savory cakes, soup, and butter. Even the shells were boiled to make a hot beverage.

The outer shell of the sunflower seed is not edible and must be stripped away to reveal the kernel. Look for raw unsalted sunflower kernels, usually available in bulk, at your specialty grocer. I don't recommend canned sunflower kernels, since they almost always are treated with MSG.

See "Notes from Ganache Hill" (page 6) for purchasing information on white chocolate.

White Chocolate Sunflower Cookies will keep for several days if stored in a tightly sealed plastic container. I don't recommend freezing this cookie.

Note: Photograph appears on page 58.

INGREDIENTS

2   cups unsalted sunflower kernels
3   cups all-purpose flour
1   teaspoon baking soda
½   teaspoon salt
4   ounces white chocolate, chopped into ¼-inch pieces
6   ounces unsalted butter, cut into 1-ounce pieces
1   cup granulated sugar
⅛   cup honey
3   large eggs
1   teaspoon pure vanilla extract

LET THE SUNFLOWERS SHINE IN

Preheat the oven to 325 degrees Fahrenheit.

Toast the sunflower kernels on a baking sheet with sides (to prevent errant kernels) for 10 minutes in the preheated oven. Cool to room temperature.

In a sifter combine the flour, baking soda, and salt. Sift onto a large piece of wax paper and set aside until needed.

Heat 1 inch of water in the bottom half of a double boiler over medium heat. With the heat on, place the white chocolate in the top half of the double boiler. Use a rubber spatula to stir the chocolate until completely melted and smooth, about 3 to 4 minutes. Transfer the melted chocolate to a 1-quart bowl and set aside until needed.

Place the butter, sugar, and honey in the bowl of an electric mixer fitted with a paddle. Beat on medium for 4 minutes. Use a rubber spatula to scrape down the sides of the bowl, then continue to beat on medium for 4 more minutes. Scrape down the bowl. Add the eggs, one at a time, beating on medium for 1 minute and scraping down the sides of the bowl after each addition. Add the vanilla extract and beat on medium for 1 minute. Stop the mixer and add the melted white chocolate and beat on medium for 1 minute. Operate the mixer on low while gradually adding the sifted dry ingredients, followed by the sunflower kernels; mix for 1 minute. Remove the bowl from the mixer and use a rubber spatula to finish mixing the dough until thoroughly combined.

Using a heaping tablespoon of dough for each cookie (approximately 1¼ ounces), portion 9 cookies, evenly spaced, onto each of 4 nonstick baking sheets. Place the baking sheets on the top and center racks of the preheated oven and bake for 10 minutes, rotating the sheets from top to center about halfway through the baking time (at that time also turn each sheet 180 degrees). Remove the cookies from the oven and cool to room temperature on the baking sheets, about 30 minutes. Store the cooled cookies in a tightly sealed plastic container until ready to serve.

CHOCOLATE "LOLLIPOPALOOZAS"
Yields 12 Lollipopaloozas

INGREDIENTS

1 cup unsalted peanuts

1½ cups granulated sugar

¼ teaspoon cream of tartar

¼ cup water

½ ounce unsweetened chocolate, chopped into ¼-inch pieces

12 ounces semisweet chocolate, chopped into ¼-inch pieces

EQUIPMENT

Measuring cups, measuring spoons, cook's knife, cutting board, 5 nonstick baking sheets, food processor with metal blade, 1½-quart saucepan, whisk, 12 popsicle sticks, metal spoon, double boiler, rubber spatula, 1-quart bowl, plastic cookie storage container with lid

THE CHEF'S TOUCH

If the popsicle sticks are not predipped and the sugar allowed to harden before proceeding, the remaining syrup will not adhere and form the lollipop.

It might take a little practice to master the technique of forming lollipops, but it's worthwhile to be one of the few people around who knows how to dish up this sweet thing.

Lollipopaloozas will keep for several days in the refrigerator in a tightly sealed plastic container.

Serve them cold directly from the fridge.

MAKE THE LOLLIPOPALOOZAS

Preheat the oven to 325 degrees Fahrenheit.

Toast the peanuts on a baking sheet in the preheated oven for 10 minutes. Cool to room temperature.

Process the peanuts in the bowl of a food processor fitted with a metal blade until finely chopped, about 8 to 10 seconds. Set aside.

Heat the sugar, cream of tartar, and water in a 1½-quart saucepan over medium-high heat. When hot, stir with a whisk to dissolve the sugar. Bring to a boil. Boil the mixture, stirring often, for 8 to 10 minutes, until the mixture takes on a light honey color. Remove the pan from the heat. Add the unsweetened chocolate and stir gently and carefully (this is very hot stuff) to incorporate.

One at a time, dip 1 inch of one end of each popsicle stick into the hot sugar mixture. Place the dipped sticks onto 4 nonstick baking sheets, leaving lots of space between sticks. Use a metal spoon to stir the mixture for 3 to 4 minutes, until it begins to get very syrupy in texture (it should still be too hot to touch or taste at this point). Pour a full tablespoon of the sugar mixture over the dipped ends of each stick, allowing the mixture to flow into a round lollipop shape. Allow the chocolate lollipops to harden at room temperature.

Heat 1 inch of water in the bottom half of a double boiler over medium heat. With the heat on, place the semisweet chocolate in the top half of the double boiler. Use a rubber spatula to stir the chocolate until completely melted and smooth, about 3 minutes. Transfer the melted chocolate to a 1-quart bowl. Place the chopped peanuts on a baking sheet. Grasp a chocolate lollipop by the stick end and dip the hardened sugar end into the chocolate to completely cover. Allow the excess chocolate to drip off before sprinkling chopped peanuts on both sides to cover the chocolate. Place the Lollipopalooza on a baking sheet. Repeat with remaining Lollipopaloozas. Refrigerate to harden the chocolate. Store in a tightly sealed plastic container in the refrigerator until ready to serve.

Celebrate!

OPPOSITE: **Black Gold Cookies (see page 101)**   ABOVE: **Mocha Meringue Morels (see page 98)**

WHITE CHOCOLATE SNOW CAPS

Yields 2½ dozen 2¼-inch cookies

INGREDIENTS

1½ cups walnut pieces
3½ cups all-purpose flour
1 teaspoon baking powder
1 teaspoon salt
⅛ teaspoon ground cardamom
6 ounces white chocolate, chopped into ¼-inch pieces
6 ounces unsalted butter, cut into 1-ounce pieces
1 cup granulated sugar
3 large eggs
1 teaspoon pure vanilla extract
¼ cup confectioners' sugar

EQUIPMENT

Measuring cups, measuring spoons, cook's knife, cutting board, 3 nonstick baking sheets, sifter, wax paper, double boiler, rubber spatula, 1-quart bowl, table-model electric mixer with paddle, plastic cookie storage container with lid

THE CHEF'S TOUCH

The Snow Caps will keep for several days at room temperature if stored in a tightly sealed plastic container. For long-term storage, up to several weeks, they may be frozen before they have been dusted with confectioners' sugar (bring frozen cookies to room temperature before dusting with the sugar). Freeze the Snow Caps in a tightly sealed plastic container to prevent dehydration and to protect them from freezer odors.

MAKE THE WHITE CHOCOLATE SNOW CAPS

Preheat the oven to 325 degrees Fahrenheit.

Toast the walnuts on a baking sheet in the preheated oven for 8 to 10 minutes. Remove the walnuts from the oven and cool to room temperature before chopping into ⅛-inch pieces with a cook's knife.

In a sifter combine the flour, baking powder, salt, and cardamom. Sift onto a large piece of wax paper and set aside until needed.

Heat 1 inch of water in the bottom half of a double boiler over medium heat. With the heat on, place the white chocolate in the top half of the double boiler. Use a rubber spatula to stir the chocolate until completely melted and smooth—"real" white chocolate should glisten when melted (see "Notes from Ganache Hill")—about 2 to 3 minutes. Transfer the melted chocolate to a 1-quart bowl and set aside until needed.

Place the butter and granulated sugar in the bowl of an electric mixer fitted with a paddle. Beat on medium for 3 minutes until soft. Use a rubber spatula to scrape down the sides of the bowl, then beat on high for 3 minutes until very smooth. Again, scrape down the bowl. Add the eggs, one at a time, beating on medium for 1 minute and scraping down the sides of the bowl after each addition. Add the vanilla extract and beat on high for 30 seconds. Stop the mixer and add the melted white chocolate, then beat on medium for 30 seconds more. Operate the mixer on low while gradually adding the sifted dry ingredients. Once all the dry ingredients have been incorporated, about 1 minute, add the chopped walnuts and mix on low for an additional 30 seconds. Remove the bowl from the mixer and use a rubber spatula to finish mixing the dough until thoroughly combined.

Using a heaping tablespoon (approximately 1½ ounces) of dough for each cookie, portion 10 cookies, evenly spaced, onto each of the 3 nonstick baking sheets. Place the baking sheets on the top and center racks of the preheated oven and bake for 16 to 18 minutes until very lightly browned around the edges, rotating the sheets from top to center halfway through the baking time (at that time also turn each sheet 180 degrees). Remove the cookies from the oven and cool to room temperature on the baking sheets, about 30 minutes. Transfer the cookies onto a large piece of wax paper. Now for that magical touch that gives the cookie its name: use a sifter to uniformly dust the tops of the cookies with the confectioners' sugar (I prefer a heavy snow to a light flurry). Store the cookies in a tightly sealed plastic container.

COCOA APRICOT CORDIAL COOKIES

Yields 3 dozen 2-inch cookies

PREPARE THE BRANDIED APRICOT FILLING

Heat the chopped apricots, the brandy, and granulated sugar in a 1½-quart saucepan over medium-high heat, stirring constantly to dissolve the sugar (careful, this blessed bouquet may make you swoon). Bring the mixture to a boil, then reduce the heat and simmer for 15 minutes until slightly thickened. Remove from the heat and transfer to a 1-quart bowl and hold at room temperature until needed.

MAKE THE COCOA COOKIES

Preheat the oven to 350 degrees Fahrenheit.

Toast the sliced almonds on a baking sheet in the preheated oven until golden brown, about 15 minutes. Remove the almonds from the oven and cool to room temperature before chopping for 10 seconds in a food processor fitted with a metal blade (you may finely chop them by hand using a cook's knife). Set aside.

In a sifter combine the flour, cocoa powder, and salt. Sift onto a large piece of wax paper and set aside until needed.

Place the butter, brown sugar, and honey in the bowl of an electric mixer fitted with a paddle. Beat on medium for 2 minutes until soft. Use a rubber spatula to scrape down the sides of the bowl, then beat on high for 1 minute until smooth. Add the egg yolks and beat on medium for 1 minute until incorporated. Scrape down the bowl. Add the almond extract and beat on high for 30 seconds. Operate the mixer on low while gradually adding the sifted dry ingredients until incorporated, about 1 minute. Remove the bowl from the mixer and use a rubber spatula to finish mixing the ingredients until thoroughly combined.

Divide the cookie dough into 36 level tablespoon–size pieces (approximately ½ ounce per piece) onto a large piece of wax paper. Gently roll each portion in the palms of your hands to form a ball, dampening your hands with water as necessary to prevent the dough from sticking. Lightly whisk together the egg whites in a small bowl. Dip the balls, one at a time, in the egg whites and then roll in the ground almonds to coat evenly. Divide the almond-coated dough balls onto 3 nonstick baking sheets, 12 evenly spaced balls per sheet. Use the back of a ½-teaspoon measuring spoon to form a shallow indentation in the center of each cookie. Place the baking sheets on the top and center racks of the preheated oven and bake for 10 to 12 minutes, rotating the sheets from top to center halfway through the baking time (at that time also turn each sheet 180 degrees). Remove the cookies from the oven and immediately fill each indentation with 1 level teaspoon of the apricot mixture. Cool to room temperature on the baking sheets, about 30 minutes. Store the cooled cookies in a tightly sealed plastic container.

INGREDIENTS

BRANDIED APRICOT FILLING

4 ounces finely chopped dried apricots
½ cup brandy
¼ cup granulated sugar

COCOA COOKIE BATTER

2 cups sliced almonds
1½ cups all-purpose flour
¼ cup unsweetened cocoa powder
½ teaspoon salt
½ pound unsalted butter, cut into 1-ounce pieces
¼ cup tightly packed light brown sugar
¼ cup honey
2 large egg yolks
½ teaspoon almond extract
2 large egg whites

EQUIPMENT

Cook's knife, cutting board, measuring cups, measuring spoons, 1½-quart saucepan, 2 1-quart bowls, 3 nonstick baking sheets, food processor with metal blade, sifter, wax paper, table-model electric mixer with paddle, rubber spatula, small whisk, plastic cookie storage container with lid

THE CHEF'S TOUCH

Jon Pierre's inspiration for this marvel was a cookie his mother made every Christmas back home in Wisconsin. She used currant jelly and walnuts to decorate the cookies.

These cookies will keep for several days at room temperature if stored in a tightly sealed plastic container, or for more than a week covered with plastic wrap in the refrigerator.

CHOCOLATE LEMON BISCOTTI

Yields 4 dozen 5-inch by 1¼-inch biscotti

INGREDIENTS

4½ cups all-purpose flour

1 tablespoon baking powder

1 teaspoon salt

1½ cups granulated sugar

½ pound unsalted butter, cut into 1-ounce pieces

4 large eggs

2 tablespoons minced lemon zest

1 teaspoon lemon extract

6 ounces semisweet chocolate, chopped into ¼-inch pieces

EQUIPMENT

Measuring cups, measuring spoons, cook's knife, cutting board, vegetable peeler, sifter, wax paper, table-model electric mixer with paddle, rubber spatula, 4 10×15-inch baking sheets, parchment paper, serrated knife, plastic cookie storage container with lid

THE CHEF'S TOUCH

A sharp vegetable peeler (a new one may be in order) is the key to properly removing only the colored part of the lemon skin and not the bitter white pith that lies directly beneath. Use a very sharp cook's knife to finely mince the skin.

The biscotti is both versatile and durable. It will keep crispy and delicious for several days on a plate at room temperature. For longer storage, up 2 to 3 weeks, store the biscotti in a tightly sealed plastic container at room temperature. The biscotti may also be frozen for several weeks stored in a tightly sealed plastic container to prevent dehydration and to protect them from freezer odors.

MAKE THE CHOCOLATE LEMON BISCOTTI

Preheat the oven to 325 degrees Fahrenheit.

In a sifter combine 4 cups flour, baking powder, and salt. Sift onto a large piece of wax paper and set aside until needed.

Place the sugar and butter in the bowl of an electric mixer fitted with a paddle. Beat on medium for 2 minutes until soft. Use a rubber spatula to scrape down the sides of the bowl, then beat on high for 4 minutes until very smooth. Add the eggs, one at a time, beating on medium for 1 minute and scraping down the sides of the bowl after each addition. Add the lemon zest and extract and beat on high for 30 seconds. Operate the mixer on low while gradually adding the sifted dry ingredients. Once all of the dry ingredients have been incorporated, about 30 seconds, turn off the mixer and add the chopped chocolate and mix on low for 30 seconds. Remove the bowl from the mixer and use a rubber spatula to finish mixing the ingredients until thoroughly combined.

Transfer the biscotti dough to a clean, dry, lightly floured work surface. Divide the dough into 4 equal portions, and shape each into a log 8 inches long, 2½ inches wide, and 1¼ inches high (using the remaining flour as necessary to prevent sticking). Carefully place 2 logs, about 2 inches apart, onto each of 2 baking sheets lined with parchment paper.

Bake the biscotti logs on the top and center racks of the preheated oven for 35 minutes, until lightly browned and firm to the touch, rotating the sheets from top to center halfway through the baking time (at that time also turn each sheet 180 degrees). Remove the logs from the oven and reduce the oven temperature to 275 degrees Fahrenheit.

Allow the logs to cool for about 15 minutes at room temperature before handling. Place the biscotti logs onto a cutting board. Using a very sharp serrated knife, trim the rounded ends from each log. Cut each biscotti log into ½-inch diagonal slices (12 slices per log). Divide the slices onto 4 baking sheets lined with parchment paper.

Bake the biscotti slices on the top and center racks of the preheated oven for 30 minutes until crisp and evenly browned, rotating the sheets from top to center halfway through the baking time (at that time also turn each sheet 180 degrees). Remove the biscotti from the oven and allow them to cool thoroughly before storing in a tightly sealed plastic container.

COCOA CORN FLOUR AND PEANUT COOKIES WITH SPICY TROPICAL FRUIT SALSA

Yields 3 dozen 2½-inch cookies and approximately 1½ quarts salsa

INGREDIENTS

SPICY TROPICAL FRUIT SALSA

2 ripe medium mangoes, peeled, pitted, and diced into ¼-inch pieces

1 ripe medium pineapple, peeled, cored, and diced into ¼-inch pieces

4 tablespoons fresh lime juice

1 teaspoon finely minced jalapeño pepper

½ teaspoon salt

COCOA CORN FLOUR AND PEANUT COOKIE BATTER

1 cup unsalted peanuts

2 cups all-purpose flour

1 cup masa harina (corn flour)

½ cup unsweetened cocoa powder

1 pound unsalted butter, cut into 1-ounce pieces

½ cup creamy peanut butter

1½ cups granulated sugar

2 large eggs

2 large egg yolks

2 teaspoons pure vanilla extract

EQUIPMENT

Paring knife, cook's knife, cutting board, measuring spoons, measuring cups, 3-quart stainless steel (or other noncorrosive) bowl, plastic wrap, 3 nonstick baking sheets, sifter, wax paper, table-model electric mixer with paddle, rubber spatula, 1-quart bowl, plastic cookie storage container with lid

PREPARE THE SPICY TROPICAL FRUIT SALSA

Combine the mango, pineapple, lime juice, jalapeño, and salt in a 3-quart stainless steel or glass bowl. Cover the bowl with plastic wrap and refrigerate for at least 1 hour before serving.

MAKE THE COCOA CORN FLOUR AND PEANUT COOKIES

Preheat the oven to 350 degrees Fahrenheit.

Toast the peanuts in the preheated oven until a light golden brown, about 8 to 10 minutes. Remove the peanuts from the oven and cool to room temperature before chopping with a cook's knife into ⅛-inch pieces. Set aside.

In a sifter combine the flour, ⅔ cup masa harina, and cocoa powder. Sift onto a large piece of wax paper and set aside until needed.

Place the butter, peanut butter, and ¾ cup granulated sugar in the bowl of an electric mixer fitted with a paddle. Beat on medium for 3 minutes until smooth. Use a rubber spatula to scrape down the sides of the bowl, then continue to beat on medium for 2 more minutes until very smooth. Then scrape down the bowl. Add the eggs and egg yolks and beat on medium for 1 minute until incorporated, then scrape down the sides of the bowl. Add the vanilla extract and beat on high for 30 seconds. With the mixer on low, gradually add the sifted dry ingredients and mix for 1 minute. Stop the mixer and add the chopped peanuts, then continue mixing until incorporated, about 30 seconds. Remove the bowl from the mixer and use a rubber spatula to finish mixing the ingredients until thoroughly combined.

Combine the remaining masa harina and sugar in a 1-quart bowl. Divide the cookie dough into 36 heaping tablespoon-size pieces (approximately 1½ ounces for each cookie) onto a large piece of wax paper. Place the dough portions, one at a time, into the sugar-and-masa-harina mixture, rolling to coat evenly. Divide the portions onto 3 nonstick baking sheets, 12 evenly spaced portions per baking sheet. Use your fingers to gently press and flatten each dough portion into a disk 3 inches in diameter and ½ inch thick. Place the baking sheets on the top and center racks of the preheated oven and bake for 10 minutes until lightly browned, rotating the sheets from top to center halfway through the baking time (at that time also turn each sheet 180 degrees). Remove the cookies from the oven and cool to room temperature on the baking sheets for about 30 minutes. Store the cooled cookies in a tightly sealed plastic container until ready to use.

TO SERVE

Portion about 4 tablespoons of salsa onto a 7-inch plate, top with 2 cookies, and serve immediately.

THE CHEF'S TOUCH

To celebrate Cinco de Mayo, which glorifies the liberation of Mexico from French colonial rule, this recipe combines chocolate (beloved of the Aztecs) with the flavors of the tropics. This sweet is particularly refreshing after dining on arroz con pollo *(and you thought I would say* mole poblano de guajolote*).*

Two medium-size fresh limes should yield the necessary 4 tablespoons of juice for the salsa.

Jalapeño peppers can be a pain—literally and figuratively—to handle. I suggest wearing plastic gloves, and avoiding contact with the seeds by using the edge of the knife to scrape them away from the inside of the pepper.

You should be able to locate masa harina (corn flour) in your local supermarket. Cornmeal is not a viable substitute.

Cocoa Corn Flour and Peanut Cookies will keep for several days at room temperature if stored in a tightly sealed plastic container. For long-term storage, up to several weeks, the cookies may be frozen in a tightly sealed plastic container to prevent dehydration and to protect them from freezer odors.

I recommend preparing the salsa on the day (perhaps the 5th of May) that you plan on serving it; otherwise, the fresh fruit flavors will taste bitter after extended storage.

CHOCOLATE KEY LIME BARS

Yields 4 dozen 1-inch bars

INGREDIENTS

CHOCOLATE CRUST

1   cup unsalted macadamia nuts

1¼ cups all-purpose flour

¾   cup confectioners' sugar

4   ounces semisweet chocolate, chopped into 1/4-inch pieces

¼   pound unsalted butter, cut into 1-ounce pieces

KEY LIME FILLING

2   cups granulated sugar

5   large eggs

½   cup fresh Key lime juice

1   tablespoon minced lime zest

¼   teaspoon salt

EQUIPMENT

Measuring cups, cook's knife, cutting board, vegetable peeler, measuring spoons, baking sheet, food processor with metal blade, sifter, 7-quart bowl, double boiler, rubber spatula, 9×13×2-inch nonstick rectangular baking pan, 4-quart bowl, whisk, 2 toothpicks, serrated knife with rounded tip, plastic cookie storage container with lid

MAKE THE CHOCOLATE CRUST

Preheat the oven to 350 degrees Fahrenheit.

Toast the macadamia nuts on a baking sheet in the preheated oven for 10 minutes. Remove the nuts from the oven and cool to room temperature.

Process the macadamia nuts in the bowl of a food processor fitted with a metal blade until finely chopped, about 8 to 10 seconds, and set aside.

In a sifter combine the flour and ½ cup of the confectioners' sugar. Sift into a 7-quart bowl. Set aside until needed.

Heat 1 inch of water in the bottom half of a double boiler over medium heat. With the heat on, place the semisweet chocolate and the butter in the top half of the double boiler. Use a rubber spatula to stir the chocolate and butter until completely melted and smooth, about 4 minutes. Transfer the melted chocolate mixture to the bowl containing the sifted dry ingredients. Add the chopped macadamia nuts and use a rubber spatula to stir the ingredients until thoroughly combined. Transfer the mixture to the 9×13×2-inch nonstick baking pan. Use your fingertips to press the mixture onto the bottom of the pan and into the corners and sides, creating an even layer.

Place the pan on the center rack of the preheated oven and bake until a toothpick inserted in the center comes out relatively clean (ever-so-slightly moist is okay), about 18 to 20 minutes. Remove the pan from the oven and hold at room temperature while making the filling.

MAKE THE KEY LIME FILLING

In a 4-quart bowl, whisk the granulated sugar, eggs, Key lime juice, lime zest, and salt. Combine thoroughly. Pour the mixture over the chocolate crust and bake on the center rack of the preheated oven until a toothpick inserted into the center comes out clean, about 30 minutes. Remove the bar from the oven and cool at room temperature for 2 hours before finishing.

TO SERVE

Place the remaining ¼ cup confectioners' sugar in a sifter. Evenly sift the sugar over the surface of the bar (if the bar is not cool, it will absorb quite a bit of the sugar). Use a serrated knife with a rounded tip to cut the Chocolate Key Lime Bar into 24 2-inch squares, then cut each square in half for 48 bars. For a clean cut, heat the blade of the knife under hot running water and wipe the blade dry before making each cut. Serve the bars immediately or store in a tightly sealed plastic container in the refrigerator.

THE CHEF'S TOUCH

Workaday limes should never be confused with Key limes. The latter, which are much smaller and yellower, are difficult to find because they are not extensively grown. Caveat emptor: few restaurants serve a true Key lime pie. Consumer advisories aside, the tiny Key lime delivers big flavor. I was awakened to the difference in 1984, when premiere confectioner Maida Heatter prepared Key lime pie for the Economic Summit attendees visiting Williamsburg; she brought Key limes with her from Florida, where they are cultivated. My friend Rolf Herion, then pastry chef for Colonial Williamsburg, told me that Mrs. Heatter was adamant about using these limes; after the first bite, we understood why she was so insistent.

Don't worry if you can't find fresh Key limes. We have found a very acceptable product marketed under the Nellie & Joe's Famous Key West Lime Juice label (it is a 100% natural juice). Otherwise, use fresh lime juice and just call the bars Chocolate Lime Bars; they will still be delicious, and you won't have to fib.

Chocolate Key Lime Bars may be eaten at room temperature, but are better after several hours of refrigeration (the chocolate crust becomes delightfully crunchy). They will keep for several days if refrigerated in a tightly sealed plastic container. After 2 to 3 days of refrigeration you may want to dust the bars with some additional confectioners' sugar.

Since you probably won't be celebrating an Economic Summit at your place anytime soon, I suggest serving these refreshing bars at your next cookout.

MOCHA MERINGUE MORELS
Yields about 3 dozen 1½-inch cookies

INGREDIENTS

1½ cups walnuts
1   tablespoon instant espresso powder
1   teaspoon pure vanilla extract
3   large egg whites
1   teaspoon cream of tartar
2½ cups confectioners' sugar
10 ounces semisweet chocolate,
    chopped into ¼-inch pieces

EQUIPMENT

Measuring cups, measuring spoons, cook's knife, cutting board, 2 baking sheets, food processor with metal blade, 2 1-quart bowls, parchment paper, table-model electric mixer with balloon whip, rubber spatula, pastry bag, double boiler, wax paper, plastic cookie storage container with lid

THE CHEF'S TOUCH

You should be able to find instant espresso powder at your specialty grocer; otherwise, you may use instant coffee (expect a less robust flavor, but no change in texture).

The meringue may be whisked by hand if you are so inclined, or use a hand-held electric mixer.

Mocha Meringue Morels will keep for 1 or 2 days if stored in a tightly sealed plastic container. Longer storage will significantly diminish the delightful crunch you get when biting into this delicacy.

Note: Photograph appears on page 87.

MAKE THE MOCHA MERINGUE MORELS

Preheat the oven to 325 Fahrenheit.

Toast the walnuts in the preheated oven for 8 minutes. Remove from the oven and cool to room temperature.

Process the walnuts in the bowl of a food processor fitted with a metal blade until finely chopped, about 8 to 10 seconds, and set aside.

Combine the espresso powder and the vanilla extract in a 1-quart bowl and stir to dissolve the espresso powder. Set aside until needed.

Line 2 baking sheets with parchment paper.

Place the egg whites and the cream of tartar in the bowl of an electric mixer fitted with a balloon whip. Whisk on high until the egg whites begin to stiffen, about 2 minutes. Add the espresso mixture and whisk on medium for 30 seconds. Operate the mixer on medium while gradually adding the confectioners' sugar until incorporated, about 1 minute. Increase the speed to high and whisk until very stiff, but not dry, peaks are formed. Remove the bowl from the mixer and use a rubber spatula to quickly fold and thoroughly combine the meringue.

Fill a pastry bag (with no tip) with the meringue. Pipe 18 evenly spaced mounds of meringue onto each parchment-lined baking sheet, creating slightly tapering cones about 1½ inches in diameter at the base and 1¾ to 2 inches high. Place the baking sheets on the center rack of the preheated oven and bake for 45 minutes. Remove the meringues from the oven and allow to cool to room temperature for 30 minutes.

Heat 1 inch of water in the bottom half of a double boiler over medium heat. With the heat on, place the semisweet chocolate in the top half of the double boiler. Use a spatula to stir the chocolate until completely melted and smooth, about 5 to 6 minutes. Transfer the melted chocolate to a 1-quart bowl. Place the chopped walnuts in a separate 1-quart bowl adjacent to the melted chocolate. Hold a baked meringue by the base and dip it into the melted chocolate, then gently shake off any excess chocolate. Roll the chocolate-coated meringue in the chopped walnuts to coat evenly and lightly. Place the Mocha Meringue Morel on a large sheet of wax paper. Repeat this procedure with the remaining meringues. Allow the Morels to stand at room temperature for 30 minutes before storing; keep the Morels in a tightly sealed plastic container until ready to serve.

CRANBERRY CHOCOLATE ITTY BITTY BISCUITS WITH CHOCOLATE BUTTER

Yields about 4½ dozen 1¾-inch biscuits

MAKE THE BISCUITS

Preheat the oven to 325 degrees Fahrenheit.

Place 3½ cups flour, the baking powder, granulated sugar, and salt in the bowl of an electric mixer fitted with a paddle. Mix on low for 30 seconds to combine the ingredients. Add the 8 tablespoons chilled butter pieces and mix on low for 2 minutes, until the butter is "cut into" the flour and the mixture develops a mealy texture. Add the buttermilk, dried cranberries, and chocolate mini-morsels and mix on low for 10 seconds. Increase the mixer speed to medium and mix until the dough comes together, about 10 seconds (be careful not to over-mix or you will have less-than-tender biscuits). Transfer the dough to a clean, dry, lightly floured work surface.

Roll the dough (using extra flour as necessary to prevent sticking) to a thickness of ¾ inch. Cut the dough into 32 biscuits using a 1½-inch biscuit cutter (occasionally dip the cutter in flour to prevent sticking). Form the remaining dough into a ball. Roll the dough to a thickness of ¾ inch. Cut the dough into 12 biscuits using the biscuit cutter. Once again, form the remaining dough into a ball. Roll the dough to a thickness of ¾ inch. Cut the dough into 12 biscuits. Divide the biscuits onto 2 nonstick baking sheets (about 28 evenly spaced biscuits per sheet). Bake the biscuits on the center rack of the preheated oven for 12 to 14 minutes, until very lightly browned. Rotate the baking sheets from one side of the oven to the other about halfway through the baking time (at that time also turn each sheet 180 degrees). Remove the biscuits from the oven. The biscuits may be served immediately, or cool for 30 minutes and store in a tightly sealed plastic container.

MAKE THE CHOCOLATE BUTTER

Place the ½ pound butter in the bowl of an electric mixer fitted with a paddle. Beat on medium for 2 minutes. Use a rubber spatula to scrape down the sides of the bowl. Add the melted chocolate and beat on high until fluffy, 4 to 5 minutes. Serve the chocolate butter with the warm biscuits.

INGREDIENTS

CRANBERRY CHOCOLATE ITTY BITTY BISCUIT BATTER

- **3¾** cups all-purpose flour
- **2** tablespoons baking powder
- **3** tablespoons granulated sugar
- **½** teaspoon salt
- **8** tablespoons chilled unsalted butter, cut into 1-tablespoon pieces
- **1¼** cups nonfat buttermilk
- **1½** cups dried cranberries
- **6** ounces semisweet chocolate mini-morsels

CHOCOLATE BUTTER

- **½** pound unsalted butter, cut into 1-ounce pieces
- **1** ounce melted semisweet chocolate

EQUIPMENT

Measuring cups, measuring spoons, table-model electric mixer with paddle, rolling pin, 1½-inch biscuit cutter, 2 nonstick baking sheets, plastic cookie storage container with lid

THE CHEF'S TOUCH

The Itty Bitty Biscuits (this diminutive, morsel actually has more in common with a buttermilk scone than a biscuit) are scrumptious the day they are baked. They can be stored for a day or two at room temperature in a tightly sealed plastic container. For that just-baked taste, warm them for 8 to 10 minutes in a 325-degree-Fahrenheit oven before serving.

Serve the biscuits warm with tea, or indulge as I do at breakfast by adding a touch of chocolate butter.

WHITE CHOCOLATE PEPPERMINT PATTIES

Yields 3 dozen 3-inch cookies

THE CHEF'S TOUCH

See "Notes from Ganache Hill" (page 6) for purchasing information on white chocolate.

Keep an eye on the cookies in the oven during baking. The cookies bake very quickly (only 9 minutes), so don't spoil the party by being distracted during the baking time.

White Chocolate Peppermint Patties will keep for several days at room temperature if stored in a tightly sealed plastic container. For long-term storage, up to several weeks, the cookies may be frozen in a tightly sealed plastic container to prevent dehydration and to protect them from freezer odors.

INGREDIENTS

¾   cup all-purpose flour
½   teaspoon baking powder
½   teaspoon salt
4   ounces white chocolate, chopped into ¼-inch pieces
½   cup granulated sugar
6   tablespoons unsalted butter
1   large egg
2   teaspoons pure vanilla extract
4   ounces peppermint candy, chopped into ⅛-inch pieces

EQUIPMENT

Measuring cups, measuring spoons, cook's knife, cutting board, sifter, wax paper, double boiler, rubber spatula, 1-quart bowl, table-model electric mixer with paddle, 3 nonstick baking sheets, plastic cookie storage container with lid

MAKE THE WHITE CHOCOLATE PEPPERMINT PATTIES

Preheat the oven to 325 degrees Fahrenheit.

In a sifter combine the flour, baking powder, and salt. Sift onto a large piece of wax paper and set aside until needed.

Heat 1 inch of water in the bottom half of a double boiler over medium heat. With the heat on, place the white chocolate in the top half of the double boiler. Use a rubber spatula to stir the chocolate until completely melted and smooth, about 4 minutes. Transfer the melted white chocolate to a 1-quart bowl and set aside until needed.

Place the granulated sugar and butter in the bowl of an electric mixer fitted with a paddle. Beat on medium for 4 minutes until smooth. Use a rubber spatula to scrape down the sides of the bowl, then continue to beat on medium for 2 more minutes until very smooth. Add the egg and the vanilla extract and beat on medium for 1 minute until incorporated. Add the melted chocolate and beat on medium for 1 minute until combined. Scrape down the bowl. Add the sifted dry ingredients and mix on low until incorporated, about 30 seconds. Add the chopped peppermint candy and mix on low until incorporated, about 30 seconds. Remove the bowl from the mixer and use a rubber spatula to finish mixing the dough until thoroughly combined.

Using a heaping tablespoon of dough for each cookie (approximately ½ ounce), portion 12 cookies, evenly spaced, onto each of 3 nonstick baking sheets. Place the baking sheets on the top and center racks of the preheated oven and bake for 9 minutes until lightly golden brown around the edges, rotating the sheets from top to center halfway through the baking time (at that time also turn each sheet 180 degrees). Remove the cookies from the oven and cool to room temperature for 30 minutes. Store the cookies in a tightly sealed plastic container until ready to serve.

BLACK GOLD COOKIES

Yields 3 dozen 2¾-inch cookies

INGREDIENTS

6 tablespoons all-purpose flour
½ teaspoon baking powder
½ teaspoon salt
10 ounces semisweet chocolate, chopped into ¼-inch pieces
2 ounces unsweetened chocolate, chopped into 1/4-inch pieces
6 tablespoons unsalted butter
2 large eggs
½ cup granulated sugar
2 teaspoons pure vanilla extract

EQUIPMENT

Measuring spoons, cook's knife, cutting board, measuring cups, sifter, wax paper, double boiler, rubber spatula, 1-quart bowl, table-model electric mixer with paddle, 3 nonstick baking sheets, plastic cookie storage container with lid

MINE THE BLACK GOLD COOKIES

Preheat the oven to 325 degrees Fahrenheit.

In a sifter combine the flour, baking powder, and salt. Sift onto a large piece of wax paper and set aside until needed.

Heat 1 inch of water in the bottom half of a double boiler over medium heat. With the heat on, place 6 ounces semisweet chocolate, the unsweetened chocolate, and butter in the top half of the double boiler. Use a rubber spatula to stir the chocolate and butter until completely melted and smooth, about 6 minutes. Transfer the melted chocolate mixture to a 1-quart bowl and set aside until needed (you're not a true chocophile if you haven't swiped at least one finger's worth of melted chocolate).

Place the eggs, sugar, and vanilla extract in the bowl of an electric mixer fitted with a paddle. Beat on medium 4 minutes until soft. Use a rubber spatula to scrape down the sides of the bowl, then continue to beat on medium for 2 more minutes. Stop the mixer, then add the melted chocolate and beat on medium for 1 minute until incorporated. Scrape down the bowl. Add the sifted dry ingredients and the remaining 4 ounces semi-sweet chocolate and mix on low until just incorporated, about 30 seconds. Remove the bowl from the mixer and use a rubber spatula to finish mixing the dough until thoroughly combined.

Using a heaping tablespoon of dough for each cookie (approximately ¾ ounce), portion 12 cookies, evenly spaced, onto each of 3 nonstick baking sheets. Place the baking sheets on the top and center racks of the preheated oven and bake for 9 to 10 minutes, rotating the sheets from top to center halfway through the baking time (at that time also turn each sheet 180 degrees). Remove the cookies from the oven and allow to cool to room temperature on the baking sheets, about 30 minutes. Store the cooled cookies in a tightly sealed plastic container until ready to serve.

THE CHEF'S TOUCH

At my house, we indulge in these dark, rich chocolate cookies (personal favorites of mine) on Christmas Day, on my birthday, on Halloween, every Saturday during football season, on the third Wednesday of every month, and—well, you get the picture. Any cookie that delivers the unequivocal flavor of chocolate the way a Black Gold Cookie does is cause for celebration itself.

I love the proportions of this cookie. For each ½ teaspoon of flour, it has two teaspoons of chocolate. With odds like that, you'll find me baking these cookies rather than panning for gold any day.

Black Gold Cookies will keep for several days in a tightly sealed plastic container at room temperature, or in the refrigerator (they're good cold, but even better at room temperature). For long-term storage, up to several weeks, these cookies may be frozen in a tightly sealed plastic container to prevent dehydration and to protect them from freezer odors. Thaw the cookies at room temperature for 15 to 20 minutes before serving. The cookies are a bit delicate, so you may want to place wax paper between the layers.

I'm so accustomed to using skim milk on my cereal that the thought of drinking whole milk seems rather indulgent. But this is, of course, a "Celebrate!" recipe, so go for it and enjoy a large glass of whole milk with these luscious cookies.

Note: Photograph appears on page 86.

PUMPKIN PECAN CHOCOLATE CHUNK FRITTERS WITH CINNAMON APPLE ICE CREAM AND CHOCOLATE CRÈME ANGLAISE

Serves 12

INGREDIENTS

CHOCOLATE CRÈME ANGLAISE

4 ounces semisweet chocolate, chopped into ¼-inch pieces

2 cups heavy cream

3 large egg yolks

4 tablespoons granulated sugar

PUMPKIN PECAN CHOCOLATE CHUNK FRITTER BATTER

¾ cup pecans

1½ cups all-purpose flour

¼ cup granulated sugar

2 tablespoons baking powder

2 tablespoons cornstarch

½ teaspoon salt

¼ teaspoon freshly grated nutmeg

1½ cups 100% natural solid pack pumpkin

¾ cup Budweiser beer

¼ cup whole milk

1 large egg

6 ounces semisweet chocolate, chopped into ¼-inch pieces

6 cups vegetable oil

CINNAMON APPLE ICE CREAM (SEE PAGE 112)

EQUIPMENT

Cook's knife, cutting board, measuring cups, measuring spoons, nutmeg grater or mill, 2 4-quart bowls, 3-quart saucepan, whisk, instant-read test thermometer, double boiler, baking sheet, 7-quart bowl, rubber spatula, deep fryer or heavy-gauge 4-quart saucepan, candy/deep frying thermometer, #50 (½-ounce) ice-cream scoop, tongs, paper towels

MAKE THE CHOCOLATE CRÈME ANGLAISE

Place 4 ounces semisweet chocolate in a 4-quart bowl and set aside.

Heat the heavy cream in a 3-quart saucepan over medium heat. Bring to a boil. While the cream is heating, whisk 3 egg yolks and 4 tablespoons sugar together in a separate 4-quart bowl. Whisk until thoroughly combined. Pour the boiling cream into the egg yolk and sugar mixture, then stir gently to combine. Return the mixture to the saucepan and heat over medium-high heat, stirring constantly. Bring to a temperature of 180 degrees Fahrenheit, about 1 minute. Pour the hot cream and egg mixture over the chopped chocolate. Stir gently (this keeps the sauce smooth) until the chocolate is thoroughly dissolved and combined. You can keep the sauce warm in a double boiler set on low while preparing the fritters. Or you can cool the sauce in an ice-water bath, then refrigerate until needed, serving the sauce cold instead of warm (I do not recommend reheating crème anglaise).

MAKE THE PUMPKIN PECAN CHOCOLATE CHUNK FRITTERS

Preheat the oven to 325 degrees Fahrenheit.

Toast the pecans on a baking sheet in the preheated oven for 5 minutes. Remove the pecans from the oven and cool to room temperature before chopping into 1/8-inch pieces with a cook's knife.

In a 7-quart bowl, combine the flour, ¼ cup sugar, baking powder, cornstarch, salt, and nutmeg.

In a 4-quart bowl, whisk together the pumpkin puree, beer, milk, and 1 egg until thoroughly combined. Add the pumpkin mixture to the dry ingredients in the 7-quart bowl. Add the 6 ounces semisweet chocolate and the pecans. Use a rubber spatula to thoroughly combine the ingredients and set aside.

Heat the vegetable oil in a deep fryer (or high-sided, heavy-duty pot) to a temperature of 350 degrees Fahrenheit. Use a #50 ice-cream scoop (or a tablespoon) to portion the batter (approximately 1¼ to 1½ ounces for each fritter). Fry the fritters in batches by dropping 6 scoops of batter into the hot oil for each batch, and frying until golden brown, about 2 to 3 minutes. Use tongs (or a slotted spoon) to remove the fritters from the hot oil and transfer to a baking sheet lined with paper towels. Allow the oil to come back to the specified temperature after frying each batch of 6 fritters. After all the fritters have been fried, place them in the preheated oven (towels and all) for 5 to 6 minutes until hot and cooked through. Serve hot.

TO SERVE

Ladle 4 tablespoons of Chocolate Crème Anglaise onto each dessert plate. Place 2 hot fritters and 1 or 2 scoops of Cinnamon Apple Ice Cream onto the sauce on each plate and serve immediately.

THE CHEF'S TOUCH

Halloween is a big deal at the Trellis. The service staff dresses in elaborate and often ingenious costumes, and prizes of gift certificates for meals at the Trellis are awarded to the best-dressed. Our pastry chef participates in the revelry by creating a dessert with the spirit of Halloween and the fall season in mind, which is how Pumpkin Pecan Chocolate Chunk Fritters came to be.

For best results, it is important to maintain the right frying temperature. Be sure to allow the oil to return to 350 degrees before frying additional batches; otherwise, the fritters will be greasy. Also, use a slotted spoon to skim the residue on top of the oil batches; this ensures clean-looking, doodad-free fritters.

Dessert fritters may be enjoyed individually like beignets. Dust liberally with confectioners' sugar, and imagine yourself in a cafe in New Orleans.

CHOCOLATE CARAMEL PUFFS

Yields 2 dozen 1½-inch puffs

PUFF DOUGH

½   cup all-purpose flour

2   tablespoons unsweetened cocoa powder

½   cup water

4   tablespoons unsalted butter

1   tablespoon granulated sugar

3   large eggs

CHOCOLATE CARAMEL GANACHE

8   ounces semisweet chocolate, chopped into ¼-inch pieces

4   ounces unsweetened chocolate, chopped into ¼-inch pieces

1½   cups heavy cream

2   tablespoons unsalted butter

½   cup granulated sugar

⅛   teaspoon fresh lemon juice

EQUIPMENT

Measuring cups, measuring spoons, cook's knife, cutting board, sifter, wax paper, 3-quart saucepan, wooden spoon, 2 nonstick baking sheets, 4-quart bowl, 1½-quart saucepan, whisk, paring knife, pastry bag, large star tip, plastic cookie storage container with lid

THE CHEF'S TOUCH

The Puffs are best eaten within 24 hours of preparation (they seem to lose their distinctive texture when held longer). Keep the filled Puffs at room temperature to maximize the flavor and texture of the ganache.

For a more elaborate dessert, consider serving 2 to 3 Puffs in a warm caramel sauce with a dollop of whipped cream.

MAKE THE PUFFS

Preheat the oven to 375 degrees Fahrenheit.

In a sifter combine the flour and cocoa powder. Sift onto a large piece of wax paper and set aside until needed.

Heat the water, 4 tablespoons butter, and 1 tablespoon sugar in a 3-quart saucepan over medium-high heat. When hot, stir to dissolve the sugar. Bring to a boil. Remove from the heat and add the sifted dry ingredients. Use a wooden spoon to stir until the mixture comes together in a ball-like shape (it should be a bit like putty at this point). Add the eggs, one at a time, stirring energetically and thoroughly incorporating each egg before adding another. Divide the dough in level tablespoons (approximately ½ ounce per puff) onto 2 nonstick baking sheets, 12 evenly spaced portions per sheet. Place the baking sheets on the top and center racks of the preheated oven and bake for 20 minutes, rotating the sheets from top to center halfway through the baking time (at that time also turn each sheet 180 degrees). Remove the puffs from the oven and cool to room temperature.

MAKE THE CHOCOLATE CARAMEL GANACHE

Place the chopped semisweet and unsweetened chocolate in a 4-quart bowl and set aside.

Heat the heavy cream and 2 tablespoons butter in a 1½-quart saucepan over medium heat. Bring to a simmer, then lower the heat to keep the cream hot, but not simmering, until needed.

Combine ½ cup sugar and the lemon juice in a 3-quart saucepan. Stir with a whisk to combine (the sugar will resemble moist sand). Caramelize the sugar for 7 to 8 minutes over medium-high heat, stirring constantly with a whisk to break up any lumps (the sugar will first turn clear as it liquefies, then light brown as it caramelizes). Remove the saucepan from the heat. Carefully pour about ⅓ of the hot cream into the caramelized sugar. Use a whisk to stir the caramel until it stops bubbling. Add the remaining cream and stir until smooth. Immediately pour the hot caramel over the chopped chocolate and allow to stand for 5 minutes before stirring with a whisk until very smooth. Refrigerate the ganache until just slightly firm but not hard (if the ganache is too firm, it will be difficult to pipe).

Using a sharp paring knife, cut each puff in half horizontally. Transfer the chilled ganache to a pastry bag fitted with a large star tip. Pipe about 1 heaping tablespoon (approximately 1 ounce) of ganache onto the bottom half of each puff, then place the top half of the puff onto each portion of ganache. Serve immediately, or store in a tightly sealed plastic container at room temperature for 12 to 24 hours.

Keep It On Ice

OPPOSITE: **White Chocolate Orange Frozen Dream Creams (see page 110)**
ABOVE: **Strawberry Ice with Cocoa Straws (see page 118)**

CHOCOLATE HAZELNUT ESPRESSO BISCOTTI WITH CHOCOLATE ESPRESSO SORBET

Yields 4 dozen 4½-inch by 1½-inch biscotti and 2 quarts sorbet

INGREDIENTS

CHOCOLATE ESPRESSO SORBET

4 ounces semisweet chocolate, chopped into ¼-inch pieces

4 ounces unsweetened chocolate, chopped into ¼-inch pieces

2 cups water

2 cups granulated sugar

1½ cups brewed espresso

1 teaspoon pure vanilla extract

CHOCOLATE HAZELNUT ESPRESSO BISCOTTI BATTER

2 cups whole hazelnuts

4½ cups all-purpose flour

3 teaspoons baking powder

1 teaspoon salt

4 ounces semisweet chocolate, chopped into ¼-inch pieces

1½ cups granulated sugar

½ pound unsalted butter, cut into 1-ounce pieces

4 large eggs

1 tablespoon hazelnut liqueur

1 large egg white

2 tablespoons finely ground espresso beans

EQUIPMENT

Cook's knife, cutting board, measuring cups, measuring spoons, coffee grinder, 4-quart bowl, 3-quart saucepan, whisk, instant-read test thermometer, ice-cream freezer, 2-quart plastic container with lid, 4 baking sheets (1 with sides), 2 large 100% cotton towels, sifter, wax paper, double boiler, rubber spatula, 2 1-quart bowls, table-model electric mixer with paddle, parchment paper, pastry brush, serrated knife, plastic cookie storage container with lid, ice-cream scoop

PREPARE THE CHOCOLATE ESPRESSO SORBET

Place 4 ounces semisweet chocolate and the unsweetened chocolate in a 4-quart bowl. Set aside until needed.

Heat the water, 2 cups of sugar, and the brewed espresso in a 3-quart saucepan over medium-high heat. When hot, stir to dissolve the sugar. Bring to a boil. Remove the boiling liquid from the heat, and immediately pour 1 cup over the chopped chocolate. Allow to stand for 5 minutes.

Whisk the chocolate mixture vigorously until perfectly smooth, about 3 to 4 minutes. Add the remaining hot liquid and whisk to incorporate. Cool in an ice-water bath, stirring constantly, to a temperature of 40 to 45 degrees Fahrenheit, about 12 minutes (the constant stirring helps reduce the temperature more quickly, and also creates utterly smooth sorbet). When cold, add the vanilla extract and stir to incorporate.

Freeze in an ice-cream freezer following the manufacturer's instructions. Transfer the semifrozen sorbet to a plastic container, securely cover, and place in the freezer for several hours before serving (the sorbet is delicious semifrozen, so don't be bashful about trying some at this point). Serve within 2 days.

MAKE THE CHOCOLATE HAZELNUT ESPRESSO BISCOTTI

Preheat the oven to 325 degrees Fahrenheit.

Toast the hazelnuts on a baking sheet with sides in the preheated oven for 20 to 25 minutes. Remove them from the oven and immediately cover with a damp towel. Invert another baking sheet over the first one to hold in the steam (this makes the nuts easier to skin). After 5 minutes, remove the skins from the nuts by placing the nuts, a few at a time, inside a folded dry towel and rubbing vigorously between the hands. Allow the nuts to cool thoroughly before chopping. Transfer the nuts to a cutting board and chop coarsely with a cook's knife. Set aside until needed.

In a sifter combine 4 cups of flour, the baking powder, and salt. Sift onto a large piece of wax paper and set aside until needed.

Heat 1 inch of water in the bottom half of a double boiler over medium heat. With the heat on, place 4 ounces semisweet chocolate in the top half of the double boiler. Use a rubber spatula to stir the chocolate until completely melted and smooth, about 1½ to 2 minutes. Transfer the melted chocolate to a 1-quart bowl and set aside until needed.

Place 1½ cups sugar and the butter in the bowl of an electric mixer fitted with a paddle. Beat on medium for 2 minutes until soft. Use a rubber spatula to scrape down the sides of the bowl, then beat on high for 4 minutes until smooth. Add the eggs, one at a time, while beating on medium for 1 minute and scraping down the sides of the bowl after each addition. Add the hazelnut liqueur and beat on high for 30 seconds. Stop the mixer and add the melted chocolate and beat on medium for 30 seconds. Operate the mixer on low while gradually adding the sifted dry ingredients. Once all the dry ingredients have been incorporated, about 30 seconds, turn off the mixer and add the chopped hazelnuts and mix on low for another 30 seconds. Remove the bowl from the mixer and use a rubber spatula to finish mixing the batter until thoroughly combined.

Transfer the biscotti dough to a clean, dry, lightly floured work surface. Divide the dough into 4 equal portions, and shape each into a log approximately 8 inches long, 2½ inches wide, and 1¼ inches high (using the remaining flour as necessary to prevent sticking). Carefully place 2 logs, about 2 inches apart, onto each of 2 baking sheets that have been lined with parchment paper. Whisk the egg white in a 1-quart bowl until foamy. Generously brush the top of each log with the foamy egg white. Lightly and evenly sprinkle the top of each log with ½ tablespoon of ground espresso beans.

Bake the biscotti logs on the top and center racks of the preheated oven for 35 minutes until lightly browned and firm to the touch, rotating the sheets from top to center halfway through the baking time (at that time also turn each sheet 180 degrees). Remove the logs from the oven and reduce the oven temperature to 275 degrees Fahrenheit. Allow the logs to cool for about 15 minutes at room temperature before handling. Place the biscotti logs onto a cutting board. Using a very sharp serrated knife, trim the rounded ends from each log. Cut each biscotti log into ½-inch diagonal slices (12 slices per log). Divide the slices onto 4 baking sheets lined with parchment paper.

Bake the biscotti slices on the top and center racks of the preheated oven for 30 minutes until crisp and evenly browned, rotating the sheets from top to center and turning each sheet 180 degrees halfway through the baking time (at that time also turn each sheet 180 degrees). Remove the biscotti from the oven and cool thoroughly before storing in a sealed plastic container.

TO SERVE

For each person, serve 2 to 3 scoops of sorbet with at least a couple of biscotti, presented in your favorite bowls.

WHITE CHOCOLATE ORANGE FROZEN DREAM CREAMS

Yields 48 ice-cream mini-sandwiches

INGREDIENTS

WHITE CHOCOLATE ORANGE ICE CREAM

1½	cups orange juice
1	cup granulated sugar
½	cup julienned orange zest
6	ounces white chocolate, chopped into ¼-inch pieces
2½	cups whole milk
1	cup heavy cream
4	large egg yolks

ORANGE COCOA COOKIE BATTER

3	cups all-purpose flour
4	tablespoons unsweetened cocoa powder
1	teaspoon salt
½	teaspoon baking soda
½	pound unsalted butter, cut into 1-ounce pieces
½	cup granulated sugar
½	cup tightly packed light brown sugar
2	large eggs
2	tablespoons minced orange zest
1	tablespoon orange liqueur

EQUIPMENT

Measuring cups, vegetable peeler, cook's knife, cutting board, measuring spoons, 3-quart saucepan, 2 4-quart bowls, instant-read test thermometer, double boiler, plastic wrap, rubber spatula, 1-quart bowl, table-model electric mixer with paddle, ice-cream freezer, 2-quart plastic container with lid, sifter, wax paper, serrated knife, 4 nonstick baking sheets, plastic cookie storage container with lid, #50 (1/2-ounce) ice-cream scoop

PREPARE THE ICE CREAM

Heat the orange juice, ½ cup granulated sugar, and the julienned orange zest in a 3-quart saucepan over medium-high heat. When hot, stir to dissolve the sugar. Bring to a boil. Allow to boil for 20 minutes until syrupy. Transfer to a 4-quart bowl and cool in an ice-water bath to a temperature of 40 to 45 degrees Fahrenheit, about 10 minutes. Cover with plastic wrap and refrigerate until needed.

Heat 1 inch of water in the bottom half of a double boiler over medium heat. With the heat on, place the white chocolate and 1 cup of the milk in the top half of the double boiler. Use a rubber spatula to stir until completely melted and smooth, about 7 to 8 minutes. Transfer the mixture to a 1-quart bowl and set aside until needed.

Heat the remaining milk, the heavy cream, and ¼ cup of granulated sugar in a 3-quart saucepan over medium-high heat. Stir to dissolve the sugar. Bring to a boil.

While the cream mixture is heating, place the egg yolks and the remaining ¼ cup granulated sugar in the bowl of an electric mixer fitted with a paddle. Beat on high for 2 minutes. Use a rubber spatula to scrape down the sides of the bowl, then beat on high until slightly thickened and lemon-colored, 2½ to 3 minutes. Timing is important. If at this point the cream has not yet started to boil, adjust the mixer speed to low and continue to mix until it does boil. If the eggs are not mixed until the point when the boiling cream is added, undesirable lumps may form.

Pour the boiling cream into the beaten egg yolks and whisk to combine. Return to the saucepan and heat over medium-high heat, stirring constantly. Bring to a temperature of 185 degrees Fahrenheit, about 1 minute. Remove from the heat and transfer to a 4-quart bowl. Add the melted white chocolate mixture and stir to combine. Cool in an ice-water bath to a temperature of 40 to 45 degrees Fahrenheit, about 20 minutes. When the mixture is cold, freeze in an ice-cream freezer according to the manufacturer's instructions. Transfer the semifrozen ice cream to a 2-quart plastic container. Use a rubber spatula to fold in the chilled orange mixture until thoroughly combined. Securely cover the container, then place in the freezer for several hours before assembling the ice-cream sandwiches.

MAKE THE COOKIES

In a sifter combine the flour, cocoa powder, salt, and baking soda. Sift onto a large piece of wax paper and set aside until needed.

Place the butter, ½ cup granulated sugar, and the brown sugar in the bowl of an electric mixer fitted with a paddle. Beat on medium for 4 minutes until fairly smooth. Use a rubber spatula to scrape down the sides of the bowl. Beat on high for 2 minutes until smooth. Scrape down the bowl again. Add the eggs, one at a time, while beating on medium for 1 minute and scraping down the sides of the bowl after each addition. Add the minced orange zest and orange liqueur and beat on high for 1 minute. Operate the mixer on low while gradually adding the sifted dry ingredients until incorporated, about 1 minute. Remove the bowl from the mixer and use a rubber spatula to finish mixing the dough until thoroughly combined.

Transfer the dough to a clean, dry, lightly floured work surface. Divide the dough into 6 equal portions, and shape each into a log approximately 10 inches long, 1½ inches wide, and ¾ inch high. Tightly wrap each log in plastic wrap. Refrigerate the logs for 4 hours until the dough is very firm.

Preheat the oven to 350 degrees Fahrenheit.

Remove the dough from the refrigerator and discard the plastic wrap. Use a sharp serrated knife to cut each log into 16 ½-inch-thick slices. Arrange the slices onto 4 nonstick baking sheets, 24 evenly spaced slices per sheet. Bake the cookies on the top and center racks of the preheated oven for 6 minutes until slightly dry in appearance, rotating the sheets from top to center halfway through the baking time (at that time also turn each sheet 180 degrees). Remove the cookies from the oven and cool to room temperature on the baking sheets, about 20 minutes. The cookies may be stored in a tightly sealed plastic container until you are ready to assemble the ice-cream sandwiches.

ASSEMBLE THE DREAM CREAMS ICE-CREAM SANDWICHES

Place 48 cookies upside down on wax paper (makes cleaning up a snap). Portion a #50 scoop (about ½ ounce) of White Chocolate Orange Ice Cream onto each of the cookies. Place a cookie, top side up, on each ice-cream scoop. Gently press the cookie into place. Serve immediately or store in a tightly sealed plastic container in the freezer.

CHOCOLATE SNICKERDOODLE ICE-CREAM SANDWICHES

Yields 18 ice-cream sandwiches

INGREDIENTS

CINNAMON APPLE ICE CREAM

2	Red Delicious apples, cored, peeled, and diced into ¼-inch pieces
1½	cups granulated sugar
2	cups half-and-half
2	cups heavy cream
6	large egg yolks
1	tablespoon pure vanilla extract
1	teaspoon ground cinnamon

SNICKERDOODLE BATTER

3	cups all-purpose flour
2	teaspoons cream of tartar
1½	teaspoons baking soda
¼	teaspoon salt
4	ounces semisweet chocolate, chopped into ¼-inch pieces
1¼	cups granulated sugar
¾	cup tightly packed light brown sugar
½	pound unsalted butter, cut into 1-ounce pieces
2	large eggs
1	teaspoon pure vanilla extract
2	teaspoons ground cinnamon

EQUIPMENT

Paring knife, cook's knife, cutting board, measuring cups, measuring spoons, 1½-quart saucepan, 2 1-quart bowls, 3-quart saucepan, table-model electric mixer with paddle, rubber spatula, whisk, instant-read test thermometer, 4-quart bowl, ice-cream freezer, 2-quart plastic container with lid, sifter, wax paper, double boiler, 3 nonstick baking sheets, plastic cookie storage container with lid, #20 (1½-ounce) ice-cream scoop

PREPARE THE CINNAMON APPLE ICE CREAM

Heat the diced apples and ½ cup granulated sugar in a 1½-quart saucepan over medium heat. Stir to dissolve the sugar. Allow the apples to cook, stirring occasionally, for 10 minutes, until slightly thickened. Remove from the heat and transfer to a 1-quart bowl. Allow to cool at room temperature while making the ice cream.

Heat the half-and-half, heavy cream, and ½ cup granulated sugar in a 3-quart saucepan over medium-high heat. When hot, stir to dissolve the sugar. Bring to a boil.

While the cream is heating, place the egg yolks and the remaining 1/2 cup of sugar in the bowl of an electric mixer fitted with a paddle. Beat on high for 2 minutes. Scrape down the sides of the bowl, then beat on high until slightly thickened and lemon-colored, about 2½ to 3 minutes. Timing is important. If at this point the cream has not yet started to boil, adjust the mixer speed to low and continue to mix until it does boil. If the eggs are not mixed until the point when the boiling cream is added, undesirable lumps may form.

Pour the boiling cream into the beaten egg yolks and whisk to combine. Return to the saucepan and heat over medium-high heat, stirring constantly—if you used a saucepan smaller than 3 quarts, you could be in trouble because the mixture expands. In any event, stir gently to avoid spillage onto your range top. Bring to a temperature of 185 degrees Fahrenheit, about 1 minute. Remove from the heat and add the vanilla extract and ground cinnamon; stir gently to incorporate. Transfer to a 4-quart bowl and cool in an ice-water bath to a temperature of 40 to 45 degrees Fahrenheit, about 15 minutes.

When the mixture is cold, freeze in an ice-cream freezer according to the manufacturer's instructions. Transfer the semifrozen ice cream to a 2-quart plastic container. Use a rubber spatula to stir in the cooked apples until thoroughly combined (we have purposely left a few spoonfuls more than needed to make the sandwiches so sample the ice cream now). Securely cover the container, then place in the freezer for several hours before assembling the ice-cream sandwiches.

MAKE THE SNICKERDOODLES

Preheat the oven to 350 degrees Fahrenheit.

In a sifter combine the flour, cream of tartar, baking soda, and salt. Sift onto a large piece of wax paper and set aside.

Heat 1 inch of water in the bottom half of a double boiler over medium heat. With the heat on, place the semisweet chocolate in the top half of the double boiler. Use a rubber spatula to stir the chocolate until completely melted and smooth, about 3 to 4 minutes. Transfer the melted chocolate to a small bowl and set aside until needed.

Place ¾ cup of the granulated sugar, the brown sugar, and the butter in the bowl of an electric mixer fitted with a paddle. Beat on medium for 2 minutes until soft. Use a rubber spatula to scrape down the sides of the bowl, then beat on high for 4 minutes until smooth. Add the eggs, one at a time, beating on medium for 1 minute and stopping to scrape down the sides of the bowl after each addition. Add the vanilla extract and beat on high for 1 minute. Stop the mixer and add the melted chocolate. Beat on medium for 30 seconds until incorporated. Operate the mixer on low while gradually adding the sifted dry ingredients. Once all the dry ingredients have been incorporated, about 30 seconds, remove the bowl from the mixer and use a rubber spatula to finish mixing the ingredients until thoroughly combined.

Combine the remaining ½ cup granulated sugar and ground cinnamon in a 1-quart bowl. Divide the dough into 36 heaping tablespoon–size pieces (approximately 1¼ ounces per piece) onto a large piece of wax paper. Gently roll each portion in the palms of your hands to form a ball (dampen your hands with water as necessary to prevent the dough from sticking). Place each ball, one at a time, into the sugar and cinnamon mixture, rolling to coat evenly. Divide the balls onto 3 nonstick baking sheets, 12 evenly spaced balls per baking sheet. Use your fingers to gently press and slightly flatten each dough ball into a disk that is 2 inches in diameter and ¾ inch thick. Place the baking sheets on the top and center racks of the preheated oven and bake for 12 to 14 minutes, rotating the sheets from top to center halfway through the baking time (at that time also turn each sheet 180 degrees). Remove the cookies from the oven and cool to room temperature on the baking sheets, about 30 minutes. Store the cooled cookies in a tightly sealed plastic container in the freezer until ready to use.

ASSEMBLE THE SNICKERDOODLE ICE-CREAM SANDWICHES

Place 18 Snickerdoodles upside down on a large piece of wax paper. Portion a #20 scoop (about 1½ ounces) of Cinnamon Apple Ice Cream onto each of the cookies. Place another cookie, top side up, on each ice-cream portion. Gently press the cookie into place. Serve immediately or store in a tightly sealed plastic container in the freezer.

CHOCOLATE- AND PEANUT-DIPPED BUTTER CUPS WITH BANANA SPLIT ICE CREAM

Yields 18 butter cups and 3 quarts ice cream

INGREDIENTS

BANANA SPLIT ICE CREAM

1   pint strawberries, stemmed and cut into ¼-inch-thick slices

1   pound bananas, peeled and cut into ¼-inch-thick slices

1   cup plus 2 tablespoons granulated sugar

2   tablespoons fresh lemon juice

3   cups heavy cream

1   cup half-and-half

4   large egg yolks

CHOCOLATE- AND PEANUT-DIPPED BUTTER CUP COOKIE BATTER

¾   cup unsalted peanuts

⅔   cup dark corn syrup

¼   cup tightly packed dark brown sugar

6   tablespoons unsalted butter

1¾ cups all-purpose flour

⅛   teaspoon baking soda

⅛   teaspoon salt

½   teaspoon pure vanilla extract

3   ounces semisweet chocolate, chopped into 1/4-inch pieces

EQUIPMENT

Cook's knife, cutting board, measuring cup, measuring spoons, 3-quart saucepan, 3-quart bowl, instant-read test thermometer, plastic wrap, table-model electric mixer with paddle, rubber spatula, whisk, 4-quart bowl, 5-quart plastic container with lid, food processor fitted with a metal blade, sifter, wax paper, rolling pin, 3½-inch round cutter, 3 standard 6-cup muffin tins, double boiler, 1-quart bowl, plastic cookie storage container with lid, #12 (2½-ounce) ice-cream scoop

MAKE THE ICE CREAM

Heat the strawberries, bananas, 2 tablespoons granulated sugar, and the lemon juice in a 3-quart saucepan over medium heat. As the mixture heats, the sugar will dissolve and the fruit will become mushy. Bring the mixture to a simmer, then reduce the heat to maintain a simmer for 10 minutes, stirring frequently until thickened. Remove the mixture from the heat and transfer to a 3-quart bowl. Cool the fruit mixture in an ice-water bath to a temperature of 40 to 45 degrees Fahrenheit, about 15 minutes. When cool, cover with plastic wrap and refrigerate until ready to use.

Heat the heavy cream, half-and-half, and ½ cup granulated sugar in a 3-quart saucepan over medium-high heat. When hot, stir to dissolve the sugar. Bring to a boil.

While the cream is heating, place the egg yolks, along with the remaining ½ cup granulated sugar, in the bowl of an electric mixer fitted with a paddle. Beat on high for 2 minutes. Use a rubber spatula to scrape down the sides of the bowl, then beat on high for 3 more minutes until slightly thickened and lemon-colored. Timing is important. If at this point the cream has not yet started to boil, adjust the mixer speed to low and continue to mix until the cream boils. If the eggs are not mixed until the boiling cream is added, undesirable lumps may form.

Pour the boiling cream into the beaten egg yolks and whisk to combine. Return the mixture to the saucepan and heat over medium-high heat, stirring constantly. Bring to a temperature of 185 degrees Fahrenheit, about 1 minute. Remove from the heat and transfer to a 4-quart bowl. Cool in an ice-water bath to a temperature of 40 to 45 degrees Fahrenheit, about 15 minutes.

When the mixture is cold, freeze in an ice-cream freezer according to the manufacturer's instructions. Transfer the semifrozen ice cream to a 5-quart plastic container. Use a rubber spatula to fold the strawberry and banana purée throughout the ice cream. Securely cover the container, then place in the freezer for several hours before serving.

MAKE THE CHOCOLATE- AND PEANUT-DIPPED BUTTER CUP COOKIES

Preheat the oven to 325 degrees Fahrenheit.

Toast the peanuts on a baking sheet in the preheated oven for 10 to 12 minutes until golden brown. Remove the nuts from the oven and cool to room temperature before finely chopping in a food processor fitted with a metal blade, about 20 seconds, or by hand using a cook's knife.

Heat the corn syrup, brown sugar, and butter in a 3-quart saucepan over medium-high heat. Bring to a boil, stirring constantly to dissolve the sugar and melt the butter. Allow to boil for 4 minutes while continuing to stir. Remove from the heat and allow to cool at room temperature to 125 degrees Fahrenheit, about 30 minutes.

In a sifter combine 1½ cups of flour, the baking soda, and salt. Sift onto a large piece of wax paper and set aside until needed.

Place the sifted dry ingredients in the bowl of an electric mixer fitted with a paddle. Add the vanilla extract to the corn syrup, sugar, and butter mixture and whisk to combine. Operate the mixer on low while gradually adding the corn syrup, butter, and sugar mixture until incorporated, about 1 minute. Use a rubber spatula to scrape down the sides of the bowl, then beat on medium until smooth, about 1 minute. Remove the dough from the mixer and transfer to a clean, dry work surface. Use your hands to flatten and form the dough into a 6×8×½-inch rectangle. Cover with plastic wrap and refrigerate for 1 hour.

Preheat the oven to 375 degrees Fahrenheit.

After 1 hour, unwrap the dough and hold at room temperature for 15 minutes. Transfer to a clean, dry, lightly floured work surface. Roll the dough (using the extra ¼ cup flour as necessary to prevent the dough from sticking) into a larger rectangle measuring 14×18 inches. Use a round cutter that is 3½ inches in diameter to cut 12 circles from the dough. Place the circles of dough onto a large piece of wax paper. Combine the scraps from the first cutting, and roll again into a rectangle, this one measuring 10×12 inches. Cut 6 more circles from the dough. Arrange the circles of dough onto the bottoms of the cups of the inverted muffin tins, pressing gently to form the dough around the cups.

Very gently pierce the dough 2 or 3 times on the bottom with a fork to prevent bubbles from forming during baking. Bake on the top and center racks of the preheated oven for 7 to 9 minutes until lightly golden brown. Remove the Butter Cup Cookies from the oven and allow to cool on the tins for 30 minutes before removing.

Heat 1 inch of water in the bottom half of a double boiler over medium heat. With the heat on, place the semisweet chocolate in the top half of the double boiler. Use a rubber spatula to stir the chocolate until completely melted and smooth, about 2 minutes. Transfer the melted chocolate to a 1-quart bowl. Place the chopped peanuts in a separate bowl adjacent to the melted chocolate. Grasp a Butter Cup Cookie by the bottom and dip about ¼ inch of the top edge into the melted chocolate. Then dip into the ground peanuts (they will adhere to the melted chocolate). Repeat until all the Butter Cups have been dipped. Transfer the Butter Cups to a large piece of wax paper until the chocolate hardens. The cookies may be stored in a tightly sealed plastic container until ready to fill with Banana Split Ice Cream.

TO SERVE

Place a #12-size scoop (about 2½ ounces) of Banana Split Ice Cream into each Butter Cup and serve immediately.

THE CHEF'S TOUCH

The temperature of the corn syrup, sugar, and butter mixture should not get much cooler than the recommended 125 degrees Fahrenheit; otherwise, it will get too tacky to incorporate into the sifted dry ingredients.

Because of the stiffness of this dough, it is necessary to use a table-model electric mixer.

Chocolate- and Peanut-Dipped Butter Cups will keep for several days at room temperature if stored in an airtight plastic container. For long-term storage, up to several weeks, the cookies may be frozen in an airtight container to prevent dehydration and to protect them from freezer odors.

If you have room in your freezer and you want to prepare everything ahead of time, you may scoop the ice cream into the Butter Cups, cover them tightly with plastic wrap, and store in the freezer until ready to serve.

The Banana Split Ice Cream freezes very hard due to the quantity of fruit purée. I suggest you place the container of ice cream in the refrigerator to soften it for about an hour before scooping. The Butter Cups may also be filled with any other flavor of ice cream, or with your favorite chocolate mousse. If you are counting calories (now there's a dirty word), then fill the Butter Cups with an assortment of fresh berries.

ROCKY MALT 'N SNOW CREAM SANDWICHES

Yields 24 ice-cream sandwiches

INGREDIENTS

MALT 'N SNOW ICE CREAM

2	cups heavy cream
2	cups whole milk
¼	cup barley malt sweetener
¼	cup unsweetened cocoa powder
6	large egg yolks
½	cup granulated sugar

ROCKY ROAD BROWNIE BATTER

3	cups pecans
6	large eggs
1	tablespoon pure vanilla extract
2½	cups granulated sugar
½	pound unsalted butter, cut into 1-ounce pieces
¾	cup unsweetened cocoa powder
2	cups all-purpose flour
4	cups miniature marshmallows

EQUIPMENT

Measuring cups, measuring spoons, 3-quart saucepan, table-model electric mixer with paddle, rubber spatula, whisk, instant-read test thermometer, 4-quart bowl, ice-cream freezer, 2-quart plastic container with lid, 2 10×15-inch baking sheets with sides, food processor with metal blade, 2 9×13×2-inch rectangular nonstick baking pans, parchment paper, 7-quart bowl, toothpick, plastic wrap, serrated knife, ice-cream paddle, plastic cookie storage container with lid

PREPARE THE SNOW CREAM

Heat the heavy cream, milk, malt sweetener, and ¼ cup cocoa powder in a 3-quart saucepan over medium-high heat. When hot, stir to dissolve the malt and cocoa powder. Bring to a boil.

While the cream is heating, place the egg yolks and ½ cup sugar in the bowl of an electric mixer fitted with a paddle. Beat on high for 2 minutes. Use a rubber spatula to scrape down the sides of the bowl, then beat on high until slightly thickened and lemon-colored, 2½ to 3 minutes. Timing is important. If at this point the cream has not yet started to boil, adjust the mixer speed to low and continue to mix until the cream boils. If the eggs are not mixed until the point when the boiling cream is added, undesirable lumps may form.

Pour the boiling cream into the beaten egg yolks and whisk to combine. Return to the saucepan and heat over medium-high heat, stirring constantly. Bring to a temperature of 185 degrees Fahrenheit, about 1 minute. Remove from the heat and transfer to a 4-quart bowl. Cool in an ice-water bath to a temperature of 40 to 45 degrees Fahrenheit, about 15 minutes. When the mixture is cold, freeze in an ice-cream freezer according to the manufacturer's instructions. Transfer the semifrozen ice cream to a 2-quart plastic container. Securely cover the container, then place in the freezer for several hours before assembling the ice-cream sandwiches.

MAKE THE ROCKY ROAD BROWNIE

Preheat the oven to 350 degrees Fahrenheit.

Toast the pecans on a baking sheet with sides in the preheated oven for 10 minutes. Cool the nuts to room temperature before finely chopping in a food processor fitted with a metal blade or by hand using a cook's knife. Set aside.

Line the bottom and 2 narrow sides of each of the 9×13×2-inch nonstick baking pans with a single sheet of parchment paper 9 inches wide and 20 inches long. Set aside.

Place the eggs and the vanilla extract in a 7-quart bowl and whisk lightly to combine.

Heat 2½ cups sugar, the butter, and ¾ cup cocoa powder in a 3-quart saucepan over medium-high heat. When hot, stir to dissolve the sugar and cocoa powder. Bring to a boil. Remove from the heat and stir gently with a whisk for 8 to 10 seconds.

Pour the hot butter mixture into the eggs and whisk to combine. Add the flour and whisk to combine. Add the pecans and the miniature marshmallows and use a rubber spatula to mix until thoroughly combined. Divide the batter between the two prepared pans and use a rubber spatula to spread in an even layer. Place the pans on the top and center racks of the preheated oven and bake until a toothpick inserted in the center comes out clean, about 25 minutes. Remove the brownie layers from the oven and allow to cool in the pans at room temperature for 1 hour.

Line the 2 10×15-inch baking sheets with parchment paper.

Remove the brownie layers from the baking pans, one at a time, by grasping the parchment paper and lifting the brownie layer out of the pan. Invert each layer onto a parchment-covered baking sheet. Remove and discard the parchment paper from the brownies. Cover each brownie with plastic wrap and freeze until ready to assemble the ice-cream sandwiches.

ASSEMBLE THE ICE-CREAM SANDWICHES

Remove the ice cream from the freezer. If the ice cream is rock hard, place it in the refrigerator to soften for 30 minutes or so. Remove the brownie layers from the freezer. Remove and discard the plastic wrap. Scoop the entire 2 quarts of Malt 'N Snow Ice Cream onto one of the inverted brownie layers. Use an ice-cream paddle (or a rubber spatula) to spread an even layer over the brownie. Invert the second brownie layer onto the ice cream, shiny baked side up, and gently press into place. Freeze for 1 hour before cutting.

Remove the brownie from the freezer and place on a clean, dry cutting board. Use a sharp serrated knife to trim the edges from the brownie to create a rectangle measuring approximately 7¾×11½ inches. Cut the rectangle into 3 strips lengthwise and then cut each strip into 4 squares. Finally, cut each square in half diagonally for 24 sandwiches. Serve immediately, or individually wrap in plastic wrap and store in a tightly sealed plastic container in the freezer.

STRAWBERRY ICE WITH COCOA STRAWS

Serves 6 to 8

INGREDIENTS

STRAWBERRY ICE

2   pints strawberries, stemmed and cut into ¼-inch slices

¾   cup granulated sugar

4   tablespoons fresh lemon juice

2   cups cold water

COCOA STRAWS

2   tablespoons cold water

1   large egg yolk

1   cup all-purpose flour

4   tablespoons chilled unsalted butter, cut into 1-tablespoon pieces

⅓   cup granulated sugar

1   tablespoon unsweetened cocoa powder

THE CHEF'S TOUCH

Be sure to wash the berries gently, but well, with a thorough spraying of warm water, then pat them dry with paper towels.

You can speed the freezing process by freezing the mixture in a shallow pan instead of a deep bowl (the downside, of course, is that the shallow pan takes up more freezer space, and makes stirring the mixture without spillage quite a challenge).

The Cocoa Straws will keep for 2 to 3 days at room temperature if stored in a tightly sealed plastic container. For long-term storage, up to several weeks, the straws may be frozen in a tightly sealed plastic container to prevent dehydration and to protect them from freezer odors.

Note: Photograph appears on page 107.

EQUIPMENT

Cook's knife, cutting board, measuring cups, measuring spoons, food processor with metal blade, 4-quart stainless steel (or other noncorrosive) bowl, whisk, metal spoon, 2-quart plastic container with lid, 1-quart bowl, table-model electric mixer with paddle, plastic wrap, rolling pin, pizza cutter, 2 nonstick baking sheets, plastic cookie storage container with lid, ice-cream scoop

MAKE THE STRAWBERRY ICE

Place the strawberries, ¾ cup sugar, and the lemon juice in the bowl of a food processor fitted with a metal blade. Process until smooth, about 30 seconds. Transfer the purée to a 4-quart noncorrosive bowl and add the 2 cups cold water. Whisk to combine. Place in the freezer. Stir the mixture every 25 to 30 minutes using a metal spoon until the mixture is slushy (that is, mostly frozen), about 5 hours. Transfer the ice to a 2-quart plastic container. Securely cover the container, then return to the freezer until ready to serve. Serve within several hours.

MAKE THE COCOA STRAWS

In a 1-quart bowl, whisk 2 tablespoons water and the egg yolk together to combine.

Place the flour in the bowl of an electric mixer fitted with a paddle. Add the butter and mix on low for 1 minute until the butter is "cut into" the flour and the mixture develops a coarse texture. Add the water and egg yolk mixture and mix on low until a loose dough comes together, about 30 seconds. Remove the dough from the mixer and form it into a smooth, round ball. Wrap in plastic wrap and refrigerate for 1 hour.

Preheat the oven to 325 degrees Fahrenheit.

Place the ⅓ cup sugar and the cocoa in a 1-quart bowl and stir to thoroughly combine.

Sprinkle half the amount of sugar and cocoa mixture onto a clean, dry work surface, covering a rectangular area measuring approximately 12 inches by 5 inches. Remove the dough from the refrigerator and discard the plastic wrap. Place the dough in the center of the sugar and cocoa mixture on the work surface. Roll the dough into a rectangle measuring approximately 12×5 inches. Use the pizza cutter to trim the uneven edges from the dough. Sprinkle the entire surface of the rolled dough with the remaining sugar and cocoa mixture. Use a pizza cutter to cut the dough lengthwise into strips that are 12 inches long and ¼ inch wide (should you get about 24). Place the strips, one at a time, on the baking sheets. Hold one end of a strip and gently twist 3 or 4 times to create a gentle spiral. Repeat with the remaining strips. Place the baking sheets on the center rack of the preheated oven and bake for 20 to 22 minutes until firm to the touch. Remove the straws from the oven and cool at room temperature for 30 minutes before storing in a tightly sealed plastic container.

To serve, place 2 scoops of the ice into each of 6 large balloon-shaped wine goblets. Garnish each portion with 2 or 3 straws and serve immediately.

SILK AND GOLD ICE CREAM
Yields 2 quarts

INGREDIENTS

SILK ICE CREAM
1   whole vanilla bean
2½ cups heavy cream
1½ cups whole milk
¾   cup granulated sugar
5   large egg yolks

BLACK GOLD COOKIES
1   dozen Black Gold Cookies (see page 101), chopped into ½-inch pieces

EQUIPMENT

Measuring cups, paring knife, cutting board, 3-quart saucepan, table-model electric mixer with paddle, rubber spatula, tongs, whisk, instant-read test thermometer, ice-cream freezer, 2-quart plastic container with lid, ice-cream scoop

MAKE THE SILK ICE CREAM

Using a sharp paring knife, split the vanilla bean in half lengthwise (a vanilla bean is about the same length and slightly thinner than a string bean). Heat the heavy cream, milk, half the amount of sugar, and the split vanilla bean in a 3-quart saucepan over medium-high heat. When hot, stir to dissolve the sugar. Bring to a boil, then adjust the heat so the mixture barely simmers.

While the cream mixture is heating, place the egg yolks and the remaining sugar in the bowl of an electric mixer fitted with a paddle. Beat on high for 2 minutes until combined. Use a rubber spatula to scrape down the sides of the bowl, then beat on high until slightly thickened and lemon-colored, about 2½ to 3 minutes. Adjust the mixer speed to low and continue to mix while preparing the vanilla bean. Timing is important—if the eggs are not mixed until the point when the hot cream is added, undesirable lumps may form.

Use a pair of tongs or a slotted spoon to remove the vanilla bean halves from the cream mixture. Use a sharp paring knife to scrape the seeds from the inside of the bean. Transfer the seeds to the cream mixture and whisk to combine. Discard the vanilla bean halves.

Pour the hot cream into the beaten egg yolks and whisk to combine. Return to the saucepan and heat over medium-high heat, stirring constantly. Bring to a temperature of 185 degrees Fahrenheit, about 3 minutes. Remove from the heat and cool the mixture in an ice-water bath to a temperature of 40 to 45 degrees Fahrenheit, about 15 minutes.

When the mixture is cold, freeze in an ice-cream freezer according to the manufacturer's instructions. Transfer the semifrozen ice cream to a 2-quart plastic container. Add the Black Gold Cookies and use a rubber spatula to fold together. Securely cover the container, then place in the freezer for several hours before serving. Serve within 5 days.

THE CHEF'S TOUCH

The Aztecs used vanilla to flavor chocolate in the equatorial areas of Central America long before Cortés arrived. At that time, chocolate was consumed as a cold beverage. Although we've added sugar and cream, good chocolate is still being flavored with real vanilla. This recipe unites our most intensely flavored chocolate cookie, the Black Gold Cookie, with a silky perfumed vanilla bean ice cream.

Some frugal chefs dry vanilla bean halves after removing the tiny seeds, using the remaining pod to flavor sugar or other ingredients. I feel that the residual flavor is minimal and that you'll lose the magic of the vanilla bean if you dry and reuse it.

If the Silk and Gold Ice Cream is too hard to scoop when removed from the freezer, place it in the refrigerator for 25 to 30 minutes. Not only will the ice cream flow from the spoon, the flavor will also intensify.

CHOCOLATE TOPSY-TURVIES WITH MELON BALL SORBET AND NO-NONSENSE PINEAPPLE

Serves 12

INGREDIENTS

MELON BALL SORBET

6 cups chopped (½-inch pieces) fresh cantaloupe

2 cups water

1½ cups granulated sugar

2 tablespoons fresh lemon juice

6 tablespoons Midori (melon liqueur)

NO-NONSENSE PINEAPPLE

4 cups chopped (¼-inch pieces) fresh pineapple

1 cup orange-flavored vodka

CHOCOLATE TOPSY-TURVY BATTER

1 ounce unsweetened chocolate, chopped into ¼-inch pieces

¾ cup all-purpose flour

½ cup tightly packed light brown sugar

¼ pound unsalted butter, cut into 1-ounce pieces

¼ cup light corn syrup

EQUIPMENT

Cook's knife, cutting board, measuring cups, measuring spoons, 7-quart bowl, 3-quart saucepan, rubber spatula, food processor with metal blade, instant-read test thermometer, ice-cream freezer, 2-quart container with lid, 1-quart stainless steel (or other noncorrosive) bowl, plastic wrap, 4-quart bowl, sifter, wax paper, 2 baking sheets, parchment paper, whisk, Midori bottle, paper towels, plastic cookie storage container with lid, ice-cream scoop

MAKE THE MELON BALL SORBET

Place the melon pieces in a 7-quart bowl. Set aside.

Heat the water, granulated sugar, and lemon juice in a 3-quart saucepan over medium-high heat. When hot, stir to dissolve the sugar. Bring to a boil and continue boiling for 10 minutes. Remove the sugar mixture from the heat and pour over the melon pieces, stirring the mixture with a rubber spatula. Steep the melon in the syrup for 30 minutes, stirring occasionally. Transfer the melon and syrup mixture to a food processor fitted with a metal blade and process for 1 minute until puréed.

Cool the purée in an ice-water bath to a temperature of 40 to 45 degrees Fahrenheit, about 15 to 20 minutes. Add the Midori to the chilled purée and stir to combine. Freeze the mixture in an ice-cream freezer according to the manufacturer's instructions. Transfer the semifrozen sorbet to a 2-quart plastic container. Securely cover the container, then place in the freezer for several hours before serving. Serve within 3 days.

MAKE THE NO-NONSENSE PINEAPPLE

Place the pineapple pieces in a 1-quart stainless steel or glass bowl. Pour the vodka over the pineapple. Tightly cover the top of the bowl with plastic wrap and hold at room temperature for 2 to 3 hours before using.

MAKE THE CHOCOLATE TOPSY-TURVIES

Preheat the oven to 325 degrees Fahrenheit.

Place the unsweetened chocolate in a 4-quart bowl. Set aside.

Sift the flour onto a large piece of wax paper and set aside until needed.

Line 2 baking sheets with parchment paper.

Heat the light brown sugar, butter, and corn syrup in a 3-quart saucepan over medium heat. Bring to a boil, stirring frequently with a whisk. Pour the boiling sugar mixture over the unsweetened chocolate, and stir with a rubber spatula until the chocolate has melted and blended into the mixture. Add the flour and stir until the batter is thoroughly combined and very smooth.

Portion 1 slightly heaping tablespoon (approximately 1¼ ounces) of batter in the center of each of the parchment paper–lined baking sheets (do not spread the batter as it will spread on its own in the oven). Bake on the center rack of the preheated oven (while baking, the batter will spread and form bursting bubbles) for 7 to 9 minutes or until the batter stops forming new bubbles. While the batter bakes, set up the "mold" for the Topsy-Turvies—actually the bottom of the Midori bottle—by placing the bottle upside down in a container that is about 8 inches deep and 6 inches wide. Then stabilize the mold with some paper towels pushed down into the container along the sides of the bottle. Set aside near the oven.

Remove one baking sheet from the oven (leave the other baking sheet in the oven with the oven door open). Immediately remove the parchment paper with the baked batter from the baking sheet. Invert (thus, "topsy-turvy") the baked batter onto the bottom of the upside-down Midori bottle. Discard the parchment paper. Allow the baked batter to form around the bottle. (If necessary, use your hands to help form the batter into an irregular cup-like shape. It is hot, but not too hot to handle if you move quickly.) Allow the cookie to harden on the bottle, about 45 seconds, before removing. Repeat this procedure with the other portion of baked batter.

Bake the remaining Topsy-Turvies, 2 at a time, following the same procedure used with the first 2 (use new parchment paper for each). Store the cooled Topsy-Turvies in a tightly sealed plastic container until ready to serve.

TO SERVE

Place a Chocolate Topsy-Turvy cookie in the center of each dessert plate. Portion 2 or 3 scoops of Melon Ball Sorbet in the center of each cookie. Equally divide the No-Nonsense Pineapple over the sorbet in each cookie. Serve immediately.

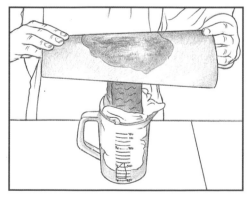

Invert the baked batter onto the bottom of the upside-down Midori bottle.

Allow the baked batter to form around the bottom of the bottle.

THE CHEF'S TOUCH

The base of the Midori bottle, with its elegantly sculpted surface and cupped bottom, yields a graceful chocolate receptacle for the sorbet, pulling extra duty out of this rather expensive melon liqueur (after all, you only use 6 tablespoons of the liqueur in the recipe).

Bottle design aside, I don't recommend any substitutes for Midori. Made from honeydew, it is the Rolls Royce of melon liqueurs, and with only 21% alcohol by volume, it delivers exquisite melon flavor.

For purchasing purposes, you should find that one medium-size (about 3¼ pounds) cantaloupe will yield 2 pounds of peeled and seeded melon, which when cut into ½-inch pieces should yield 6 cups.

Select a medium-size (about 2 pounds) pineapple. It should yield the necessary 4 cups of ½-inch pineapple pieces.

Keep the kids or the abstemious away from the No-Nonsense Pineapple. The alcohol does not evaporate as it does if it were heated, so you'll be serving spiked pineapple. I used orange-flavored vodka as a take on the Melon Ball cocktail recipe, which includes orange juice and vodka. You may want to experiment with other flavored vodkas.

The Topsy-Turvies are very susceptible to humidity. Store them in a tightly sealed plastic container in a cool (not refrigerated) dry place. Shelf life will depend on the temperature and humidity in your home.

More Than a Mouthful

OPPOSITE: **Golden Spider Webs with Wicked Ganache and Raspberry Rapture (see page 139)**
ABOVE: **Chocolate Heavenly Bodies (see page 140)**

DEEP-DISH PIZZA COOKIE

Yields 16 1½-inch-wide-by-4-inch-long slices of pizza cookie

INGREDIENTS

WHITE CHOCOLATE PIZZA CRUST

3	cups all-purpose flour
1	teaspoon baking powder
½	teaspoon salt
4	ounces white chocolate, chopped into ¼-inch pieces
4	tablespoons granulated sugar
2	large egg yolks
1	teaspoon pure vanilla extract
12	ounces chilled unsalted butter, cut into 1-ounce pieces

PIZZA TOPPING

1	cup pecans
1	cup heavy cream
¼	cup tightly packed light brown sugar
2	cups dried cranberries
4	ounces finely diced dried apricots
4	ounces semisweet chocolate, chopped into ¼-inch pieces
2	ounces white chocolate, chopped into ¼-inch pieces

EQUIPMENT

Measuring cups, measuring spoons, cook's knife, cutting board, sifter, wax paper, double boiler, rubber spatula, 1-quart bowl, 4-quart bowl, whisk, table-model electric mixer with paddle, 9×3-inch springform pan, baking sheet, 3-quart saucepan, serrated knife, plastic cookie storage container with lid

MAKE THE WHITE CHOCOLATE PIZZA CRUST

Preheat the oven to 375 degrees Fahrenheit.

In a sifter combine the flour, baking powder, and salt. Sift onto a large piece of wax paper and set aside until needed.

Heat 1 inch of water in the bottom half of a double boiler over medium heat. With the heat on, place 4 ounces white chocolate in the top half of the double boiler. Use a rubber spatula to stir the chocolate until completely melted and smooth, about 4 minutes. Transfer the chocolate to a 1-quart bowl. In a 4-quart bowl whisk together the granulated sugar, egg yolks, and vanilla extract until combined and the sugar has dissolved. Add the melted white chocolate and whisk to combine. Set aside.

Place the sifted dry ingredients and butter in the bowl of an electric mixer fitted with a paddle. Mix on low for 2 minutes until the butter is "cut into" the flour and the mixture develops a coarse, mealy texture. Add the white chocolate mixture to the flour-and-butter mixture and mix on low for 30 seconds until a loose dough is formed. Transfer the dough to a clean, dry work surface and knead gently to form a smooth dough. Place the dough in the springform pan and use your fingers to press the dough first into the bottom and then three quarters of the way up the sides of the pan. Place the pan on the center rack of the preheated oven and bake for 14 minutes. Remove the pan from the oven and allow to stand at room temperature while preparing the topping.

PREPARE THE PIZZA TOPPING
Preheat the oven to 375 degrees Fahrenheit.

Toast the pecans on a baking sheet in the preheated oven for 5 minutes. Remove the pecans from the oven and cool to room temperature before chopping into ¼-inch pieces with a cook's knife.

Heat the heavy cream and light brown sugar in a 3-quart saucepan over medium heat. When hot, stir to dissolve the sugar. Bring to a boil, then adjust the heat and allow to simmer for 6 minutes until slightly thickened. Remove from the heat and add the dried cranberries, apricots, and toasted pecans; stir with a rubber spatula to combine. Transfer the dried-fruit-and-nut mixture to the crust, using a rubber spatula to spread the topping evenly over the crust. Sprinkle the chopped semisweet chocolate evenly over the entire surface of the topping. Place the pan on the center rack of the preheated oven and bake for 30 minutes until lightly browned around the edges. Remove the pizza from the oven and allow to cool to room temperature for 1 hour.

Heat 1 inch of water in the bottom half of a double boiler over medium heat. With the heat on, place 2 ounces white chocolate in the top half of the double boiler. Use a rubber spatula to stir the chocolate until completely melted and smooth, about 3 minutes. Use a teaspoon to drizzle thin lines of white chocolate over the entire surface of the pizza topping. Allow the chocolate to become firm at room temperature before cutting.

Remove the pizza from the pan and place on a cutting board. Use a serrated knife to cut the pizza into 16 1½-inch-wide slices. Store the pizza cookies in a tightly sealed plastic container until ready to serve.

THE CHEF'S TOUCH

I worried that my assistant Jon Pierre Peavey was spending too much time at Pizzeria Uno when he suggested we create a deep-dish pizza cookie for this book. But then I realized that "More Than a Mouthful" was the perfect place to showcase a cookie homage to one of my favorite foods, pizza.

Since the pecans are chopped, you can save some money by buying pecan pieces rather than the more expensive pecan halves.

See "Notes from Ganache Hill" (page 6) for purchasing information on white chocolate.

I find the balance of fruit and nuts to be perfect in this recipe; and just like I love anchovies on my savory pizza, you can be creative and experiment with other dried fruits and nuts.

The whole pizza, as well as the pizza slices, may be stored in a tightly sealed plastic container for several days or more.

CHOCOLATE COOKIE CABINS
Serves 6

INGREDIENTS

COCOA MERINGUE LOGS

3 tablespoons unsweetened cocoa powder

2 tablespoons cornstarch

7 large egg whites

¼ teaspoon cream of tartar

⅛ teaspoon salt

1½ cups confectioners' sugar

10 ounces semisweet chocolate, chopped into ¼-inch pieces

WHITE CHOCOLATE MORTAR

½ pound white chocolate, chopped into ¼-inch pieces

3 cups heavy cream

DARK CHOCOLATE ROOF

3 ounces semisweet chocolate, grated

"NEIGE"

½ cup confectioners' sugar

EQUIPMENT

Measuring spoons, measuring cups, cook's knife, cutting board, box grater, 4 baking sheets, parchment paper, sifter, wax paper, table-model electric mixer with balloon whip, rubber spatula, pastry bag, double boiler, 4-quart bowl, 7-quart bowl, whisk, plastic wrap

MAKE THE COCOA MERINGUE LOGS

Preheat the oven to 200 degrees Fahrenheit.

Line 4 baking sheets with parchment paper. Set aside.

In a sifter combine the cocoa powder and corn starch. Sift onto a large piece of wax paper and set aside until needed.

Place the egg whites, cream of tartar, and salt in the bowl of an electric mixer fitted with a balloon whip. Whisk on high until soft peaks form, about 1 minute. Gradually add the confectioners' sugar while whisking on medium. Whisk until stiff, but not dry, about 1 minute. Stop the mixer, add the sifted dry ingredients, and whisk on medium for 30 seconds until incorporated. Remove the bowl from the mixer and use a rubber spatula to thoroughly combine the ingredients.

Fill a pastry bag with the meringue. Pipe 72 4×1-inch meringue logs onto the parchment paper–lined baking sheets (18 evenly spaced logs per sheet). Place the baking sheets on the top and center racks of the preheated oven and bake for 2 hours until dry and crisp. Remove the meringues from the oven and allow to cool for 30 minutes before handling.

Heat 1 inch of water in the bottom half of a double boiler over medium heat. With the heat on, place 10 ounces semisweet chocolate in the top half of the double boiler. Use a rubber spatula to stir the chocolate until completely melted and smooth, about 5 minutes. Transfer the melted chocolate to a 4-quart bowl.

Remove the meringue logs from the parchment paper (handle gently as the meringues are brittle). Line the baking sheets with new sheets of parchment paper. One at a time, dip each end of the cocoa meringue logs in the melted chocolate to coat about ¾ inch of each end. Return the meringues to the parchment-lined baking sheets (once again, 18 evenly spaced logs per baking sheet). Allow the chocolate to firm up at room temperature, about 30 minutes, or refrigerate for about 10 minutes.

PREPARE THE WHITE CHOCOLATE MORTAR

Heat 1 inch of water in the bottom half of a double boiler over medium heat. With the heat on, place the white chocolate in the top half of the double boiler. Use a rubber spatula to stir the chocolate until completely melted and smooth, about 4 minutes. Transfer the chocolate to a 7-quart bowl.

Place the heavy cream in the well-chilled bowl of an electric mixer fitted with a well-chilled balloon whip. Whisk on high until stiff, about 1 minute. Transfer about ¼ of the whipped cream into the melted white chocolate. Vigorously whisk by hand until combined. Add the remaining whipped cream and use a rubber spatula to quickly fold together until combined. Transfer the White Chocolate Mortar to a 4-quart bowl, cover with plastic wrap, and refrigerate for at least 1 hour before assembling the cookie cabin.

ERECT THE COOKIE CABIN

Form a V in the center of each of the dessert plates with 2 of the meringue logs (at the open end, the V should be as wide as the length of a log). At the point where the logs touch, lift one chocolate end on top of the other. Place a third meringue log onto the chocolate dipped tips of the open end of the V, creating a triangle. Continue stacking the meringues in this manner until 10 meringues have been used on each plate (because some of the logs may break during construction, this recipe includes 12 additional logs).

Transfer the White Chocolate Mortar to a pastry bag without a tip. Pipe approximately 1/6 the total amount of mortar into the center of each stack of logs and finish by creating a cone-shaped "roof" at the top of each meringue cookie stack. Sprinkle 2 tablespoons of grated chocolate over the roof of each cabin. For the final touch, let it "snow": sift an equal amount of confectioners' sugar over each cabin. Serve immediately.

This construction project will actually be completed on time, and you should have no trouble finding volunteers to clean up the construction site. Get everyone involved in raising the roof and you will be the most popular foreman in town.

Use the large holes of a box grater to grate the chocolate. Although you can grate 1-ounce baking chocolate bars, a larger block of chocolate is easier to handle.

If a table-model electric mixer is not available, both the Cocoa Meringue Logs and the White Chocolate Mortar may be whisked with a hand-held electric mixer or with a balloon whisk (mixing time will increase).

The chocolate dipped Cocoa Meringue Logs will keep for several days in a tightly sealed plastic container in the refrigerator. If you are not into the construction business, enjoy the Logs as cookies all by themselves.

CHOCOLATE BALLOON CUPS WITH OVEN-ROASTED PEARS, TOASTED HAZELNUTS, AND "BURNT" CARAMEL SABAYON

Serves 8

INGREDIENTS

BALLOON CUPS

16 ounces semisweet chocolate, chopped into ¼-inch pieces

OVEN-ROASTED PEARS AND HAZELNUTS

2 cups hazelnuts
12 ripe pears, unpeeled
1 cup honey
6 tablespoons hazelnut liqueur

"BURNT" CARAMEL SABAYON

1½ cups granulated sugar
½ teaspoon fresh lemon juice
⅓ cup heavy cream
4 large egg yolks
2 tablespoons hazelnut liqueur

EQUIPMENT

Cook's knife, cutting board, measuring cups, measuring spoons, 4 nonstick baking sheets with sides, parchment paper, 16 heavy-duty ("water-bomb") balloons, double boiler, rubber spatula, 2 4-quart bowls, instant-read test thermometer, spearpoint paring knife, large flat plastic container with lid, 2 large 100%-cotton towels, plastic wrap, 3-quart saucepan, whisk, 1-quart bowl

PREPARE THE BALLOON CUPS

Line 2 baking sheets with parchment paper.

Inflate the balloons to approximately 4-inches in diameter and securely knot each one.

Heat 1 inch of water in the bottom half of a double boiler over medium heat. With the heat on, place the semisweet chocolate in the top half of the double boiler. Use a rubber spatula to stir the chocolate until completely melted and smooth, about 7 minutes. Transfer the melted chocolate to a 4-quart bowl, and continue to stir until the temperature of the chocolate is reduced to 90 degrees Fahrenheit.

Holding an inflated balloon by the knotted end, dip about 2 to 2½-inches of the opposite end into the melted chocolate, rocking the balloon back and forth to create a cup with a scalloped effect. While continuing to hold the balloon by the knotted end, allow any excess chocolate to drip from the balloon, then place the balloon, knotted end straight up, onto a parchment paper-lined baking sheet. Repeat this procedure with the remaining 15 balloons, distributing the chocolate-dipped balloons, evenly spaced, onto 2 baking sheets. After all the balloons have been dipped, refrigerate them for 30 minutes to harden the chocolate (it may take longer for the chocolate to harden depending upon the air circulation in your refrigerator as well as the prevailing weather conditions).

Remove the chocolate-dipped balloons from the refrigerator, then deflate the balloons by popping each balloon with the pointed tip of a paring knife. Allow to stand at room temperature for 10 minutes before carefully removing the deflated balloon remnants from the inside of each chocolate cup. Be certain to discard balloon remnants, especially if you have young children in your household.

Place the chocolate balloon cups in a tightly sealed plastic container (or cover with plastic wrap) in the refrigerator until ready to serve.

PREPARE THE OVEN-ROASTED PEARS AND HAZELNUTS

Preheat the oven to 325 degrees Fahrenheit.

Toast the hazelnuts on a baking sheet with sides in the preheated oven for 20 to 25 minutes. Remove the nuts from the oven and immediately cover with a damp towel. Invert another baking sheet over the first one to hold in the steam (this makes the nuts easier to skin). After 5 minutes, remove the skins from the nuts by placing small quantities inside a folded dry towel and rubbing vigorously between your hands. Allow the nuts to cool thoroughly before chopping. Transfer the nuts to a cutting board and chop coarsely with a cook's knife. Set aside until needed.

Core and quarter the pears (do not peel). Cut the pear quarters widthwise into ½-inch-thick slices. Combine the pear slices and honey in a 4-quart bowl and use a rubber spatula to mix until the pears are thoroughly coated with the honey. Divide the pears, in a single layer, onto each of 4 nonstick baking sheets with sides (if the pears are crowded on the baking sheet, they will not roast properly). Roast the pears in the preheated oven for 20 minutes until a light golden brown. Remove the pears from the oven and cool at room temperature for 30 minutes. Transfer the pears to a 4-quart bowl. Sprinkle 6 tablespoons hazelnut liqueur over the pears. Tightly cover the top of the bowl with plastic wrap and refrigerate until ready to serve.

PREPARE THE "BURNT" CARAMEL SABAYON

Place 1 cup sugar and the lemon juice in a 3-quart saucepan and stir with a whisk to combine (the sugar will resemble moist sand). Slowly caramelize the sugar by heating for 8½ to 9 minutes over medium heat, stirring constantly with a whisk to break up any lumps until it is a deep chestnut color (the sugar will first turn clear as it liquefies, then light brown as it caramelizes). Remove the saucepan from the heat and carefully (to avoid splattering) add the cream. Stir vigorously with a whisk to combine. Transfer the "burnt" caramel sauce to a 1-quart bowl and set aside while preparing the sabayon.

Heat 1 inch of water in the bottom half of a double boiler over medium heat. With the heat on, place the egg yolks, remaining ½ cup sugar, and 2 tablespoons hazelnut liqueur in the top half of the double boiler. Vigorously whisk until soft peaks form and the mixture becomes light and airy, about 8 minutes. Remove from the heat and continue to whisk while gradually adding the "burnt" caramel sauce until thoroughly combined.

TO SERVE

Portion 4 tablespoons of "Burnt" Caramel Sabayon onto each dessert plate. Place 2 chocolate balloon cups onto the sabayon in the center of each plate. Remove the pears from the refrigerator. Use a rubber spatula to stir the pears before portioning about ¼ cup into each chocolate cup. Sprinkle an equal amount of chopped hazelnuts on top of the pears in each cup and serve immediately.

CHOCOLATE CHIP COCOA FLAPJACK STACKS WITH WARM STRAWBERRIES, CHOCOLATE SYRUP, AND TOASTED PECAN MAPLE CREAM

Serves 8

INGREDIENTS

TOASTED PECAN MAPLE CREAM

1½ cups pecan halves
½ cup heavy cream
1 tablespoon pure maple syrup
1 teaspoon pure vanilla extract

CHOCOLATE SYRUP

6 ounces semisweet chocolate, chopped into 1-ounce pieces
½ cup heavy cream
½ cup pure maple syrup
4 tablespoons unsalted butter
1 teaspoon pure vanilla extract

WARM STRAWBERRIES

4 tablespoons unsalted butter
2 tablespoons granulated sugar
2 pints strawberries, stemmed and sliced into ¼-inch pieces
¼ teaspoon freshly grated nutmeg

CHOCOLATE CHIP COCOA FLAPJACKS

2 cups all-purpose flour
4 tablespoons unsweetened cocoa powder
2 tablespoons baking powder
2 tablespoons granulated sugar
½ teaspoon salt
1½ cups whole milk
2 large eggs
6 ounces semisweet chocolate mini-morsels

EQUIPMENT

Measuring cups, measuring spoons, cook's knife, cutting board, paring knife, nutmeg grater, nonstick baking sheet, food processor with metal blade, table-model electric mixer with balloon whip, rubber spatula, 1-quart bowl, plastic wrap, 3-quart saucepan, whisk, double boiler, sifter, wax paper, 7-quart bowl, 2 large nonstick sauté pans or flat-top griddle, spatula

PREPARE THE TOASTED PECAN MAPLE CREAM

Preheat the oven to 325 degrees Fahrenheit.

Toast the pecan halves on a baking sheet in the preheated oven for 8 minutes. Remove the nuts from the oven and set aside and cool to room temperature. Reserve 1 cup of pecan halves to garnish the dessert plates. Place the remaining ½ cup pecans (be sure they are cool) in the bowl of a food processor fitted with a metal blade. Process until finely chopped, about 15 seconds. Set aside.

Place ½ cup heavy cream, 1 tablespoon maple syrup, and 1 teaspoon vanilla extract in the well-chilled bowl of an electric mixer fitted with a well-chilled balloon whip. Whisk on high until stiff, about 1½ minutes. Remove the bowl from the mixer, add the finely chopped pecans, and use a rubber spatula to fold together until combined. Transfer the Toasted Pecan Maple Cream to a 1-quart bowl, cover with plastic wrap, and refrigerate until needed.

MAKE THE CHOCOLATE SYRUP

Heat the semisweet chocolate, ½ cup heavy cream, ½ cup maple syrup, and 4 tablespoons butter in a 3-quart saucepan over medium heat. When hot, stir with a whisk to melt the chocolate. Bring to a boil, then lower the heat and allow the mixture to simmer for 5 minutes. Remove from the heat and add 1 teaspoon vanilla extract, whisking to combine. Transfer the syrup to the top of a double boiler set over low heat to keep warm until ready to serve.

PREPARE THE WARM STRAWBERRIES

Heat 4 tablespoons butter and 2 tablespoons sugar in a 3-quart saucepan over medium heat, constantly stirring to dissolve the sugar. When the mixture begins to bubble, add the strawberries and heat until warmed through, about 2 minutes. Use a rubber spatula to gently stir the berries while heating. Remove from the heat and stir in the grated nutmeg. Cover the pan and set aside while making the flapjacks.

MAKE THE CHOCOLATE CHIP COCOA FLAPJACKS

Preheat the oven to 200 degrees Fahrenheit.

In a sifter combine the flour, cocoa powder, baking powder, 2 tablespoons sugar, and salt. Sift onto a large piece of wax paper and set aside until needed.

In a 7-quart bowl, whisk together the whole milk and eggs until combined. Add the sifted dry ingredients and use a rubber spatula to stir until blended. Add the chocolate mini-morsels and stir to combine.

Heat 2 large nonstick sauté pans over medium heat until hot. Using 1 tablespoon of batter for each flapjack, portion 4 evenly spaced flapjacks per pan and cook for 1 minute until the exposed surface of each flapjack is covered with bubbles. Use a spatula to turn each flapjack over and cook for an additional 30 seconds. Transfer the flapjacks to a non-stick baking sheet and hold in the preheated oven while preparing the remaining flapjacks. Repeat until all the flapjacks have been cooked. Hold the flapjacks in the oven until ready to serve, up to 20 minutes.

ASSEMBLE THE FLAPJACK STACKS

Reheat the berries, uncovered, over low heat until warm. Place a stack of 6 flapjacks in the center of each warm dessert plate. Portion 3 to 4 tablespoons of warm berries around each stack of flapjacks. Spoon 3 to 4 tablespoons of Chocolate Syrup over the top of each stack allowing the syrup to flow freely over and down the stack. Sprinkle an equal amount of toasted pecan halves around each stack, and finally place a large dollop of Toasted Pecan Maple Cream on the top of each stack. Serve immediately.

CHOCOLATE MANGO AMBUSH
Serves 6

INGREDIENTS

WHITE CHOCOLATE ORANGE ICE CREAM (SEE PAGE 110)

MANGO AMBUSH

- 1   small mango, pitted, peeled, and cut into large chunks
- 2   tablespoons dark rum

MACADAMIA COOKIE BATTER

- ½   cup macadamia nuts
- ¼   pound unsalted butter, cut into 1-ounce pieces
- ¼   cup granulated sugar
- ¼   cup light corn syrup
- ½   teaspoon pure vanilla extract
- ⅔   cup all-purpose flour

ORANGE COCONUT CAKES

-     vegetable oil spray
- 1¾   cups all-purpose flour
- ¾   teaspoon baking powder
- ¾   teaspoon baking soda
- ½   teaspoon salt
- ½   pound unsalted butter, cut into 1-ounce pieces
- 1   cup granulated sugar
- 2   large eggs
- 1   tablespoon pure vanilla extract
- 6   ounces frozen coconut, drained
- ¼   cup orange juice
- 2   tablespoons minced orange zest
- ½   cup hot water
- ½   cup sour cream

WHITE CHOCOLATE COCONUT COATING

- 6   ounces frozen coconut, drained
- ½   pound white chocolate, chopped into ¼-inch pieces
- ½   cup heavy cream

GOLDEN CUPS

- 1   cup granulated sugar
- ¼   teaspoon fresh lemon juice

CHOCOLATE AUREOLES

- 8   ounces semisweet chocolate, chopped into ¼-inch pieces

COCOA RUM SAUCE

- 6   tablespoons unsalted butter
- ¾   cup granulated sugar
- ¾   cup heavy cream
- 6   tablespoons unsweetened cocoa powder
- ¼   teaspoon salt
- 2   tablespoons dark rum
- 1   teaspoon pure vanilla extract

EQUIPMENT

Measuring spoons, measuring cups, cook's knife, cutting board, vegetable peeler, medium-gauge strainer, food processor with metal blade, 2 1-quart bowls (1 noncorrosive), plastic wrap, 3 baking sheets with sides, parchment paper, table-model electric mixer with paddle, rubber spatula, offset cake spatula, 4½-inch round pastry cutter, 2 plastic cookie storage containers with lids, 6 8-ounce ovenproof soufflé cups, sifter, wax paper, toothpick, cooling rack, serrated knife or slicer, #20 (1½ ounce) ice-cream scoop, 2 4-quart bowls, 1½-quart saucepan, whisk, 3-quart saucepan, double boiler, instant-read test thermometer, 3½-inch round pastry cutter, 2-inch round pastry cutter,

PREPARE THE WHITE CHOCOLATE ORANGE ICE-CREAM RECIPE

Make the ice cream, then place in an ice-cream freezer until solid (depending on the freezer, somewhere between 12 and 24 hours) before serving the Chocolate Mango Ambush.

PREPARE THE MANGO AMBUSH

In the bowl of a food processor fitted with a metal blade, process the mango with 2 tablespoons dark rum for 15 seconds, until it is a chunky purée. Transfer the chunky mango purée to a 1-quart stainless steel or glass bowl. Tightly cover the bowl with plastic wrap and refrigerate until ready to serve.

MAKE THE MACADAMIA COOKIES

Preheat the oven to 325 degrees Fahrenheit.

Toast the macadamia nuts on a baking sheet in the preheated oven until golden brown, about 10 minutes. Cool the macadamia nuts to room temperature before coarsely chopping in a food processor fitted with a metal blade for 15 seconds (you may also coarsely chop the nuts by hand using a cook's knife). Set aside.

Line 2 baking sheets with parchment paper.

Place ¼ pound butter, ¼ cup sugar, and the corn syrup in the bowl of an electric mixer fitted with a paddle. Beat on medium for 4 minutes until soft. Use a rubber spatula to scrape down the sides of the bowl. Add ½ teaspoon vanilla extract and beat on high for

30 seconds. Add the chopped macadamia nuts and beat on high for 30 seconds. Scrape down the bowl. Add ⅔ cup flour and mix on low for 30 seconds until incorporated. Remove the bowl from the mixer and use a rubber spatula to finish mixing the batter until it is thoroughly combined.

Using 2 heaping tablespoons (approximately 2½ ounces) of the batter for each cookie, portion 1 cookie in the center of each of the 2 parchment-lined baking sheets. Use a cake spatula to spread the batter into a circle about 4 inches in diameter (the batter will spread during baking). Bake both sheets on the center rack of the preheated oven for 22 minutes until lightly golden brown around the edges. Remove the cookies from the oven. Immediately use a 4½-inch round pastry cutter to cut out each cookie into an identical circle. Remove the outer portion of the cookie and discard (right into your mouth is good). Allow the cookies to cool at room temperature while baking the remaining cookies.

Prepare 4 more cookies following the same procedure as with the first batch, baking 2 cookies at a time on clean parchment paper. A second oven can be used if available, but whether in one oven or two, for best results be certain to bake the cookies on the center rack. Once all the cookies have been baked and cooled, they may be stored in a tightly sealed plastic container at air-conditioned room temperature. They will stay crisp for several days.

PREPARE THE ORANGE COCONUT CAKES

Preheat the oven to 325 degrees Fahrenheit.

Prepare 6 8-ounce ovenproof soufflé cups by evenly coating the inside of each with vegetable oil spray.

In a sifter combine 1¾ cups flour, baking powder, baking soda, and ½ teaspoon salt. Sift onto a large piece of wax paper and set aside until needed.

Place ½ pound butter and 1 cup sugar in the bowl of an electric mixer fitted with a paddle. Beat on medium for 5 minutes until fairly smooth. Use a rubber spatula to scrape down the sides of the bowl. Add the eggs, one at a time, beating on medium for 1 minute and scraping down the bowl after each addition. Add 1 tablespoon vanilla extract and beat on high for 1 minute. Scrape down the bowl. Add 6 ounces coconut, orange juice, and orange zest and beat on medium for 30 seconds until incorporated. Operate the mixer on low while gradually adding the sifted dry ingredients until incorporated, about 30 seconds. Add the hot water and sour cream and beat on medium for 1 minute. Remove the bowl from the mixer and use a rubber spatula to finish mixing the batter until thoroughly combined.

Evenly divide the cake batter into the prepared soufflé cups. Place the soufflé cups on a baking sheet with sides and bake on the center rack of the preheated oven until a toothpick inserted into the center comes out clean, about 45 minutes. Remove the cakes from the oven and cool for 20 minutes before removing the cakes from the soufflé cups.

THE CHEF'S TOUCH

Chocolate Mango Ambush was the result of a challenge to create a dessert as a finale to a spectacular dinner benefiting the James Beard Foundation and the Philadelphia Academy of Vocal Arts. Each course, prepared by a well-known chef, was paired with performances by the country's most talented opera singers. To meet such a creative challenge, I brainstormed with Trellis Pastry Chef Kelly Bailey to compose a dessert with visual drama (the aureoles), chocolate (of course), and a surprise (the ambush).

I recommend tackling this dessert over the course of several days. The White Chocolate Orange Ice Cream can be prepared several days in advance. I suggest preparing the Mango Ambush a few hours prior to serving. The Orange Coconut Cakes can be baked, cooled, and refrigerated for 2 to 3 days prior to coating with the White Chocolate Coconut Coating and creating the Golden Cups; after these last two stages, the cakes can be held for several hours at room temperature before serving. The Chocolate Aureoles will keep in the refrigerator for several days. Make the Cocoa Rum Sauce the day before, then cool and refrigerate it until ready to warm in a double boiler.

After removing the cakes from the soufflé cups, place them on a cooling rack to cool completely, about 1 hour.

Use a serrated knife to trim the rounded tops from each cake to create a flat surface. Using a #20 ice-cream scoop, scoop out a hollow 2 inches in diameter and 1 inch deep from the center of the top of the cake. Set the cakes aside.

PREPARE THE WHITE CHOCOLATE COCONUT COATING

Preheat the oven to 325 degrees Fahrenheit.

Toast 6 ounces coconut on a baking sheet with sides in the preheated oven until lightly golden brown, about 20 to 22 minutes. Remove from the oven and allow to cool to room temperature while making the white chocolate ganache.

Make the ganache by placing the white chocolate in a 4-quart bowl. Set aside. Heat ½ cup heavy cream in a 1½-quart saucepan over medium heat. Bring to a boil. Pour the boiling cream over the white chocolate and set aside for 5 minutes. Use a whisk to stir until smooth. Refrigerate the ganache for 15 to 20 minutes until slightly firm but not hard.

Use a cake spatula to coat the sides of each cake with a thin layer of white chocolate ganache (about 2 level tablespoons of ganache for each cake). Place the toasted coconut in a 4-quart bowl. Roll the sides of each cake in the toasted coconut to coat evenly and lightly all the way around.

PREPARE THE GOLDEN CUPS

Place 1 cup sugar and the lemon juice in a 3-quart saucepan. Stir with a whisk to combine (the sugar will resemble moist sand). Caramelize the sugar by heating for 4½ to 5 minutes over medium-high heat, stirring constantly with a whisk to break up any lumps (the sugar will first turn clear as it liquefies, then light brown as it caramelizes). Remove the saucepan from the heat. Immediately portion about 1½ tablespoons of caramelized sugar in the hollow of each cake. Pick up a cake, then quickly and carefully, rotate it to allow the sugar to coat the entire surface of the hollow, up to the top inside edge to create a cup. Repeat this procedure until the inside hollow of each cake has been coated with golden sugar. Set aside for the golden sugar to harden.

MAKE THE CHOCOLATE AUREOLES

Line a baking sheet with parchment paper.

Heat 1 inch of water in the bottom half of a double boiler over medium heat. With the heat on, place the semisweet chocolate in the top half of the double boiler. Use a rubber spatula to stir the chocolate until completely melted and smooth, about 4 minutes. Transfer the melted chocolate to a 4-quart bowl, and stir until the chocolate reaches a temperature of 90 degrees Fahrenheit. Pour the chocolate onto the parchment-lined baking sheet, and use an offset cake spatula to spread it in an even layer over the entire surface of the parchment paper. Place the sheet in the refrigerator for 7 to 8 minutes, until the chocolate gets slightly firm but not hard. Remove the sheet from the refrigerator and use a 3 ½-inch round pastry cutter to cut 6 evenly spaced circles into the chocolate. Now use a 2-inch round pastry cutter to cut a circle in the center of each of the larger circles. Refrigerate the chocolate until it is hard, about 10 to 15 minutes. Remove the baking sheet from the refrigerator. Remove the Chocolate Aureoles from the parchment paper on the baking sheet (use the tip of a paring knife to separate the outer chocolate ring, the aureole, from the smaller inner circle, if necessary). Save the remaining chocolate inner circles and other trimmings to melt for decorating the Macadamia Cookies. Store the Chocolate Aureoles, each separated from the other by a small piece of wax paper, in a tightly sealed plastic container in the refrigerator until ready to serve.

DECORATE THE MACADAMIA COOKIES

Heat 1 inch of water in the bottom half of a double boiler over medium heat. With the heat on, place chocolate trimmings from the aureoles in the top half of the double boiler. Use a rubber spatula to stir the chocolate until completely melted and smooth, about 2 minutes. Transfer the melted chocolate to a 1-quart bowl.

Arrange the macadamia cookies close together on a piece of wax paper or parchment paper. Drizzle about 1 tablespoon of melted chocolate in thin lines onto the top of each cookie (you'll have a spoonful or two of melted chocolate to spare). Allow the cookies to set at room temperature for 25 to 30 minutes to firm the chocolate. Store in a tightly sealed plastic container until ready to serve.

MAKE THE COCOA RUM SAUCE

Heat 6 tablespoons butter, ¾ cup sugar, ¾ cup heavy cream, cocoa powder, and ¼ teaspoon salt in a 3-quart saucepan over medium heat. When hot, stir with a whisk to combine the ingredients and dissolve the sugar. Bring to a boil, then lower the heat and simmer for 5 minutes, stirring occasionally. Remove the saucepan from the heat. Add 2 tablespoons dark rum and 1 teaspoon vanilla extract and whisk to combine. Transfer the sauce to a double boiler to keep warm until ready to serve or if not using right away, cool in an ice-water bath. Store in a tightly sealed plastic container in the refrigerator until ready to serve. Warm the sauce in a double boiler before serving.

ASSEMBLE THE AMBUSH

Spoon 4 tablespoons of Cocoa Rum Sauce onto each dessert plate. Position an Orange Coconut Cake onto the sauce in the center of each plate. Portion 2 tablespoons of Mango Ambush into the Golden Cup of each cake. Center a Macadamia Cookie on the top of each cake. Place a #20 scoop of White Chocolate Orange Ice Cream onto the center of each Macadamia Cookie. Top each scoop of ice cream with a Chocolate Aureole. Serve immediately.

CHOCOLATE PALETTES
Serves 8

INGREDIENTS

PALETTE COOKIE BATTER
½ pound unsalted butter
1 cup granulated sugar
¼ teaspoon salt
6 large egg whites
½ teaspoon pure vanilla extract
2 cups all-purpose flour
1½ tablespoons unsweetened
    cocoa powder

DARK CHOCOLATE TRUFFLES
8 ounces semisweet chocolate,
   chopped into ¼-inch pieces
4 ounces unsweetened chocolate,
   chopped into ¼-inch pieces
⅔ cup heavy cream
2 tablespoons unsweetened cocoa
   powder, sifted
2 tablespoons confectioners' sugar,
   sifted

CHOCOLATE PAINT BRUSHES
16 Cocoa Straws (see page 118)
3 ounces semisweet chocolate,
   chopped into ¼-inch pieces

FRUIT GARNISH
1 pint fresh red raspberries
4 whole kiwi fruit, peeled and cut
   into 16½-inch slices

EQUIPMENT
Measuring cups, measuring spoons, cook's knife, cutting board, sifter, wax paper, paring knife, 8-inch plate, pencil, lightweight cardboard, X-Acto knife, table-model electric mixer with paddle, rubber spatula, 1-quart bowl, 4 baking sheets, parchment paper, cake spatula, 1¼-inch round pastry cutter, plastic cookie storage container with lid, 4-quart bowl, 1½-quart saucepan, plastic container with lid, double boiler, instant-read test thermometer, food processor with metal blade, medium-gauge strainer, 1-pint noncorrosive bowl, plastic wrap

PREPARE THE PALETTE COOKIES
Preheat the oven to 300 degrees Fahrenheit.

Make a template of a painter's palette. Using an 8-inch plate as a guide, trace a circle with a pencil on a 10-inch square piece of light cardboard. Create the handle for the palette by drawing a 2-inch long loop (1 ½ inches wide on the outside of the loop and 1 inch wide on the inside [need illustrations]) anywhere inside the edge of the circle. Use a sharp X-Acto knife to cut along the outline of the palette. Remove and discard the palette-shaped cutout; the outer piece of cardboard is the template.

To make the cookie batter, place the butter, granulated sugar, and salt in the bowl of an electric mixer fitted with a paddle. Beat on medium for 2 minutes until soft. Use a rubber spatula to scrape down the sides of the bowl. Beat on high for 1 minute until fairly smooth. Scrape down the sides of the bowl. Add the egg whites, one at a time, beating on high for 1 minute and scraping down the bowl after each addition. Add the vanilla extract and beat on medium for 30 seconds. Add the flour and beat on low for 15 seconds, then on medium for 10 seconds until incorporated. Remove the bowl from the mixer and use a rubber spatula to finish mixing the batter until thoroughly combined.

Transfer ½ cup of the batter to a 1-quart bowl. Add 1½ tablespoons cocoa powder and stir with a rubber spatula until thoroughly blended.

Line 4 baking sheets with parchment paper.

Center the template on a parchment-lined baking sheet. Place 3 slightly heaping tablespoons (approximately 2¾ ounces) of the plain batter in the center of the palette outline. Use a cake spatula to smear a thin coating of batter to completely cover the inside of the template (scrape away any excess batter on the cardboard surface of the template).

Carefully lift the template away from the palette-shaped batter. Repeat this procedure to form 3 more palettes on the remaining 3 parchment-lined baking sheets.

Using a clean cake spatula, randomly smear 2 level teaspoons (approximately ½ ounce) of the cocoa batter over the surface of each palette-shaped portion of batter, creating a marbleized effect. Place the baking sheets on the top and center racks of the preheated oven and bake for 17 to 18 minutes until light golden brown, rotating the sheets halfway through the

Created by Trellis Pastry Chef Kelly Bailey for a dinner at the James Beard House in New York City, the Chocolate Palettes had the right touch of whimsy to culminate an evening of serious dining. Although I had prepared dinners at the Beard House before, this was the first time I shared the stage with other chefs, all of whom were from Virginia. By mutual decision, I "drew" dessert, but it was Kelly's idea to create a visual and edible panoply instead of a single item. It was an artful and delicious idea.

As the artist, you may want to serve additional sweets on the palette, such as scoops of ice cream, pieces of brittle, praline, or other chunks of chocolate. Also, just as artists' palettes come in many shapes, you can change the shape of your palettes to suit your creativity.

It is good insurance to bake all the batter into extra palettes since they break easily.

Use the best quality chocolate available for the truffles as the chocolate is the star in this confection.

Bake the entire recipe for the Cocoa Straws. Although the recipe makes 20, possible breakage and the eating of 1 or 2 may deplete your supply.

Make sure the Palettes are sufficiently baked; otherwise, they will not stay crisp.

If a table-model electric mixer is not available, the Palette Cookie batter may be mixed with a hand-held electric mixer, or by hand with a balloon whisk (mixing time may increase). Use room-temperature butter if using either method.

The Chocolate Palette Cookies will keep for several days at room temperature in a tightly sealed plastic container.

baking time (at that time also turn each sheet 180 degrees). Remove the palette cookies from the oven, and immediately use a 1¼-inch round pastry cutter to cut a "thumbhole" (position the hole to the left or right of the indentation about 1 inch from the indentation and the edge of the palette) through the surface of the cookie (this must be done as soon as the cookies exit the oven or they will become too firm and break apart).

Remove the circle from the "thumbhole" and eat it before someone else beats you to it. Remove the parchment paper with the baked cookie to a clean, dry work surface to cool for 30 minutes at room temperature.

Line the 4 baking sheets with parchment paper and repeat the procedure used to make the first batch of palette cookies. Once all the palette cookies have been baked and cooled, store them in a tightly sealed plastic container (place a piece of parchment paper or wax paper between the cookies) at room temperature until needed (they should stay crisp for several days in a tightly sealed container at air-conditioned room temperature).

Make a template of a painter's palette.

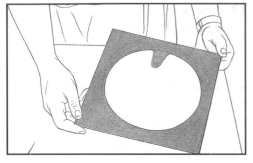

The outer piece of cardboard is the template.

Use a cake spatula to smear a thin coating of batter to completely cover the inside of the template.

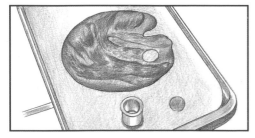

Use a 1½-inch round pastry cutter to cut a thumbhole through the surface of the cookie.

MAKE THE DARK CHOCOLATE TRUFFLES

Place 8 ounces semisweet chocolate and the unsweetened chocolate in a 4-quart bowl.

Heat the heavy cream in a 1½-quart saucepan over medium heat. Bring to a boil. Pour the boiling cream over the chocolate. Allow to stand for 5 minutes, then stir until smooth. Refrigerate the ganache for 1 hour until firm, but not hard.

Line a baking sheet with parchment paper. Using a tablespoon of ganache for each truffle (approximately ¾ ounce), portion 24 truffles, evenly spaced, onto the parchment-lined baking sheet. Refrigerate the ganache portions for 15 minutes. When the ganache is firm enough to handle, remove from the refrigerator and individually roll each portion of ganache in your palms in a gentle circular motion, using just enough pressure to form smooth rounds. Roll 16 of the rounds in 2 tablespoons cocoa powder and the remaining 8 rounds in the confectioners' sugar until completely covered. Store the truffles in a tightly sealed plastic container in the refrigerator. Remove from the refrigerator about 1 hour before serving.

PREPARE THE CHOCOLATE PAINT BRUSHES

Line 2 baking sheets with parchment paper.

Heat 1 inch of water in the bottom half of a double boiler over medium heat. With the heat on, place 3 ounces semisweet chocolate in the top half. Use a rubber spatula to stir the chocolate until completely melted and smooth, about 3 minutes. Transfer the melted chocolate to a 1-quart bowl. Now stir the melted chocolate until the temperature is reduced to 90 degrees Fahrenheit.

One at a time, dip 1½ inches of one end of each cocoa straw into the melted chocolate, rotating the tip of the straw in the chocolate to achieve an even coating. Place the dipped straws on the parchment-lined baking sheets and allow to set at room temperature for 30 minutes.

PREPARE THE FRUIT GARNISH

In the bowl of a food processor fitted with a metal blade, process ½ pint fresh red raspberries until liquefied, about 30 seconds. Strain the purée through a medium-gauge strainer into a 1-pint stainless steel or glass bowl (this should yield ½ cup smooth purée). Cover the bowl with plastic wrap and refrigerate until needed.

ASSEMBLE THE PALETTES

Place a cocoa-coated truffle in the center of each dessert plate (I suggest a 12-inch plate). Center a palette leaning up against each truffle, creating a slight incline. Drizzle 1½ to 2 teaspoons of raspberry purée in an eclectic fashion on each palette. Arrange 2 paintbrushes on each palette. Randomly place 1 confectioners' sugar–coated truffle, 1 cocoa-coated truffle, and 2 slices of kiwi on each palette. Sprinkle some of the whole raspberries onto each palette. Serve immediately.

GOLDEN SPIDER WEBS WITH WICKED GANACHE AND RASPBERRY RAPTURE

Serves 6

PREPARE THE GOLDEN SPIDER WEBS

Line 2 baking sheets with parchment paper.

Place 1 cup sugar and the lemon juice in a 3-quart saucepan. Stir with a whisk to combine (the sugar will resemble moist sand). Caramelize the sugar by heating for 4½ to 5 minutes over medium-high heat, stirring constantly with a whisk to break up any lumps (the sugar will first turn clear as it liquefies, then light brown as it caramelizes). Remove the saucepan from the heat. Allow the caramelized sugar to stand at room temperature for about a minute. Using 3 to 4 spoonfuls for each spider web, dip an oval soup spoon into the caramelized sugar and drizzle the hot sugar in a thin stream onto the parchment-lined baking sheet, creating 6 free-form, evenly spaced, 4-inch-diameter, spider-web–like designs on each sheet. Allow the spider webs to harden at room temperature. Store the Golden Spider Webs, each separated by wax paper, in a tightly sealed plastic container.

PREPARE THE WICKED GANACHE

Place the semisweet chocolate in a 4-quart bowl.

Heat the heavy cream, 2 tablespoons sugar, butter, and black pepper in a 3-quart saucepan over medium-high heat. When hot, stir to dissolve the sugar. Bring to a boil. Pour the boiling cream over the chopped chocolate. Allow to stand for 5 minutes, then stir until smooth. Place the ganache in the refrigerator for 45 minutes until firm, but not hard.

MAKE THE RASPBERRY RAPTURE

Place the fresh red raspberries in a 4-quart stainless steel or glass bowl. Use a slotted spoon to crush the berries into a rough-textured consistency. Tightly cover the top of the bowl with plastic wrap and refrigerate until ready to serve.

PREPARE THE SPIDER'S LAIR

Remove the Wicked Ganache from the refrigerator and transfer to a pastry bag fitted with a plain tip. Pipe an open circle approximately 3 inches in diameter and 1 inch high onto the center of each dessert plate. (If the ganache becomes too firm to pipe, set aside at room temperature until pipeable.) Fill each circle with 1 heaping tablespoon of the Raspberry Rapture. Position a Golden Spider Web over each circle of ganache. Pipe a second ganache circle, similar to the first, onto each spider web. Fill each ganache circle with 1 tablespoon of the raspberries. Top each circle with a Golden Spider Web. Equally divide the remaining crushed raspberries in an enticing fashion around each spider's lair. Serve immediately.

Drizzle the hot sugar in a thin stream.

INGREDIENTS

GOLDEN SPIDER WEBS
- **1** cup granulated sugar
- **¼** teaspoon fresh lemon juice

WICKED GANACHE
- **12** ounces semisweet chocolate, chopped into ¼-inch pieces
- **¾** cup heavy cream
- **2** tablespoons granulated sugar
- **4** tablespoons unsalted butter
- **2** teaspoons freshly ground black pepper

RASPBERRY RAPTURE
- **2** pints fresh red raspberries

EQUIPMENT

Measuring cups, measuring spoons, cook's knife, cutting board, 2 baking sheets, parchment paper, 3-quart saucepan, whisk, oval soup spoon, wax paper, plastic container with lid, 2 4-quart bowls (1 noncorrosive), slotted spoon, plastic wrap, pastry bag with medium plain tip

THE CHEF'S TOUCH

Don't be intimidated by the intricate appearance of this fantastical dessert—making it is not as difficult a task as it seems.

Spinning the golden webs will become second nature to you after you have practiced it a couple of times. Once you are an accomplished web spinner, you may want to keep a supply of Golden Spider Webs on hand (the better to attract your next victim).

Note: Photograph appears on page 122.

CHOCOLATE HEAVENLY BODIES
Serves 8

INGREDIENTS

GOLDEN STAR DUST
1 cup granulated sugar
¼ teaspoon fresh lemon juice

MOON AND STAR COOKIE BATTER
2 ounces semisweet chocolate, chopped into ¼-inch pieces
6 ounces unsalted butter, cut into 1-ounce pieces
1 cup granulated sugar
¼ teaspoon salt
4 large egg whites
2 tablespoons dark crème de cacao
1¾ cups all-purpose flour

ETHEREAL CLOUDS
3 cups heavy cream
¼ cup granulated sugar
2 tablespoons dark crème de cacao

EQUIPMENT

Measuring cups, measuring spoons, cook's knife, cutting board, 3-quart saucepan, whisk, 4 nonstick baking sheets with sides, food processor with metal blade, plastic container with lid, pencil, lightweight cardboard, X-Acto knife, double boiler, rubber spatula, 1-quart bowl, table-model electric mixer with paddle and balloon whip, parchment paper, cake spatula, wax paper, large flat plastic container with lid

MAKE THE GOLDEN STAR DUST

Place 1 cup of sugar and the lemon juice in a 3-quart saucepan. Stir with a whisk to combine (the sugar will resemble moist sand). Caramelize the sugar by heating for 4½ to 5 minutes over medium-high heat, stirring constantly with a whisk to break up any lumps (the sugar will first turn clear as it liquefies, then light brown as it caramelizes). Remove the saucepan from the heat and pour the caramelized sugar onto a nonstick baking sheet with sides (the hot sugar will spread over much of the sheet). Allow the caramelized sugar to cool and harden at room temperature for 30 minutes. Use your hands to break the hardened caramelized sugar into 3- to 4-inch-long, irregularly shaped pieces. Process the hardened sugar pieces in the bowl of a food processor fitted with a metal blade until very finely chopped, about 1 minute. Store the Golden Star Dust in a tightly sealed plastic container in the freezer until ready to use.

CREATE THE MOON AND STAR COOKIES

Preheat the oven to 300 degrees Fahrenheit.

Make a template of a crescent-shaped moon and a separate template of a star. Creatively trace a crescent-shaped moon and a star with a pencil on separate pieces of 5×7-inch lightweight cardboard. Cut along the outline of each using a sharp X-Acto knife (remove the cutouts); the outer pieces of cardboard with the crescent moon–shaped hole and star-shaped hole are the templates.

Heat 1 inch of water in the bottom half of a double boiler over medium heat. With the heat on, place the semisweet chocolate in the top half of the double boiler. Use a rubber spatula to stir the chocolate until completely melted and smooth, about 3 minutes. Transfer the melted chocolate to a 1-quart bowl and set aside until needed.

Place the butter, 1 cup sugar, and the salt in the bowl of an electric mixer fitted with a paddle. Beat on medium for 4 minutes until fairly smooth. Use a rubber spatula to scrape down the sides of the bowl. Add the egg whites, one at a time, beating on medium for 1 minute and scraping down the bowl after each addition. Then add the 2 tablespoons dark crème de cacao and beat on high for 1 minute. Add the melted chocolate and beat on medium for 30 seconds. Scrape down the bowl. Operate the mixer on low while gradually adding the flour until incorporated, about 30 seconds. Remove the bowl from the mixer and use a rubber spatula to finish mixing the batter until thoroughly combined.

Line 2 baking sheets with parchment paper. Place the crescent moon template on the parchment paper so that it touches one of the inside corners of the baking sheet. Place 1 level tablespoon (approximately ½ ounce) of the batter in the center of the moon outline.

Use a cake spatula to smear a thin coating of batter to completely cover the inside of the template (scrape away any excess batter on the cardboard surface of the template).

Carefully lift the template away from the moon-shaped batter. Repeat this process to form 3 more moons, one at a time, in the 3 remaining corners of the baking sheet. Then repeat to form 4 more moons on the second baking sheet. Bake both sheets on the center rack of the preheated oven for 6 to 8 minutes, until lightly browned around the edges.

While the moon cookies are baking, cut 12 more pieces of parchment paper to fit the insides of the baking sheets.

Remove the moon cookies from the oven. Immediately sprinkle ¼ teaspoon of Golden Star Dust over the surface of each Moon Cookie. Remove the parchment paper with the cookies to a clean, dry surface. Allow to cool at room temperature while baking the star cookies.

Prepare the star-shaped cookies using the same procedure used with the moon cookies, baking 16 cookies at a time, 4 each on 4 baking sheets, placing 2 sheets on the top rack and 2 sheets on the center rack of the preheated oven (line the baking sheets with unused parchment paper for each batch of cookies). Repeat this process 2 more times to create a total of 48 stars.

Once all the star cookies have been baked, sprinkled with Golden Star Dust, and cooled, store them and the moon-shaped cookies (all in layers separated by wax paper) in a tightly sealed plastic container at room temperature until needed. They will stay crisp for several days in a tightly sealed container at air-conditioned room temperature.

PREPARE THE ETHEREAL CLOUDS

Place the heavy cream, ¼ cup sugar, and 2 tablespoons dark crème de cacao in the well-chilled bowl of an electric mixer fitted with a well-chilled balloon whip. Whisk on high until stiff, about 1 minute.

TO SERVE

Spoon 4 heaping tablespoons of the Ethereal Clouds onto each chilled dessert plate. Arrange 1 crescent moon–shaped cookie and 6 star-shaped cookies on the top of the clouds, standing each vertically. Sprinkle some of the remaining Golden Star Dust over the entire plate. Serve immediately.

THE CHEF'S TOUCH

Create heaven on earth by floating these delicate chocolate moons and stars on puffs of whipped cream. As you and your guests orbit around this dessert, marveling at the beauty of this recipe's Golden Star Dust, you may wonder how you could ever face another store-bought confection.

If you would rather navigate the galaxy without the crème de cacao, you may omit it from both the cookie batter and the Ethereal Clouds without any adverse results (albeit with a tad less taste).

Also, virtually any shape can be created from a template, so don't limit yourself by just shooting for the stars.

The Moon and Star Cookies will keep for 2 to 3 days at room temperature if stored in a tightly sealed plastic container. These whimsical cookies are delicate, so handle carefully. If you must stack them in the container, I suggest you layer them between sheets of wax paper or parchment paper.

Note: Photograph appears on page 123.

Make a template of a crescent-shaped moon and a separate template of a star.

BIBLIOGRAPHY

Amendola, Joseph. *The Bakers Manual for Quantity Baking and Pastry Making*. New York: Aherns Publishing Company, Inc., 1960.

Ayto, John. *The Diner's Dictionary: Food and Drink from A to Z*. Oxford and New York: Stewart, Tabori & Chang, 1988.

Baggett, Nancy. *The International Cookie Cookbook*. New York: Stewart, Tabori & Chang, 1988.

Beranbaum, Rose Levy. *Rose's Christmas Cookies*. New York: William Morrow and Company, 1990.

Bloom, Carol. *The International Dictionary of Desserts, Pastries, and Confections*. New York: Hearst Books, 1995.

Braker, Flo. *The Simple Art of Perfect Baking*. New York: William Morrow and Company, 1985.

Desaulniers, Marcel. *Death by Chocolate*. New York: Rizzoli, 1992.

Desaulniers, Marcel. *Desserts To Die For*. New York: Simon & Schuster, 1995.

Etlinger, Steven, and Irena Chalmers. *The Kitchenware Book*. New York: Macmillan Publishing Company, 1993.

Healy, Bruce. *The French Cookie Book*. New York: William Morrow and Company, 1994.

Herbst, Sharon Tyler. *The New Food Lover's Companion*. New York: Barron's, 1995.

Knight, John B. *Knight's Foodservice Dictionary*. New York: Van Nostrand Reinhold, 1987.

Malgieri, Nick. *How To Bake*. New York: Harper Collins, 1995.

Mariani, John. *The Dictionary of American Food & Drink*. New Haven and New York: Ticknor & Fields, 1983.

Mimifie, Bernard W. *Chocolate, Cocoa, and Confectionery: Science and Technology*. New York: Van Nostrand Reinhold, 1989.

Neil, Marion H. *Candies and Bonbons and How To Make Them*. Philadelphia: David McKay, Publisher, 1913.

INDEX